THE CLONE WARS

SHIPYARDS OF DOOM

DESIGNER **KRYSTAL HENNES**

ASSISTANT EDITOR **FREDDYE LINS**

ASSOCIATE EDITOR **DAVE MARSHALL**

EDITOR **RANDY STRADLEY**

PUBLISHER **MIKE RICHARDSON**

Special thanks to Elaine Mederer, Jann Moorhead, David Anderman, Leland Chee, Sue Rostoni, and Carol Roeder at Lucas Licensing.

STAR WARS: THE CLONE WARS — SHIPYARDS OF DOOM

ISBN: 9781848561304

Published by Titan Books, a division of Titan Publishing Group Ltd.
144 Southwark St, London, SE1 OUP

A CIP catalogue record for this title is available from the British Library.

First edition: November 2008

10 9 8 7 6 5 4 3 2 1

Printed in Lithuania

 The events in these stories take place sometime during the Clone Wars.

THE CLONE WARS

SHIPYARDS OF DOOM

SCRIPT **HENRY GILROY**   ART **THE FILLBACH BROTHERS**

COLOURS **RONDA PATTISON**   LETTERING **MICHAEL HEISLER**

COVER ART **SCOTT HEPBURN**

TITAN BOOKS

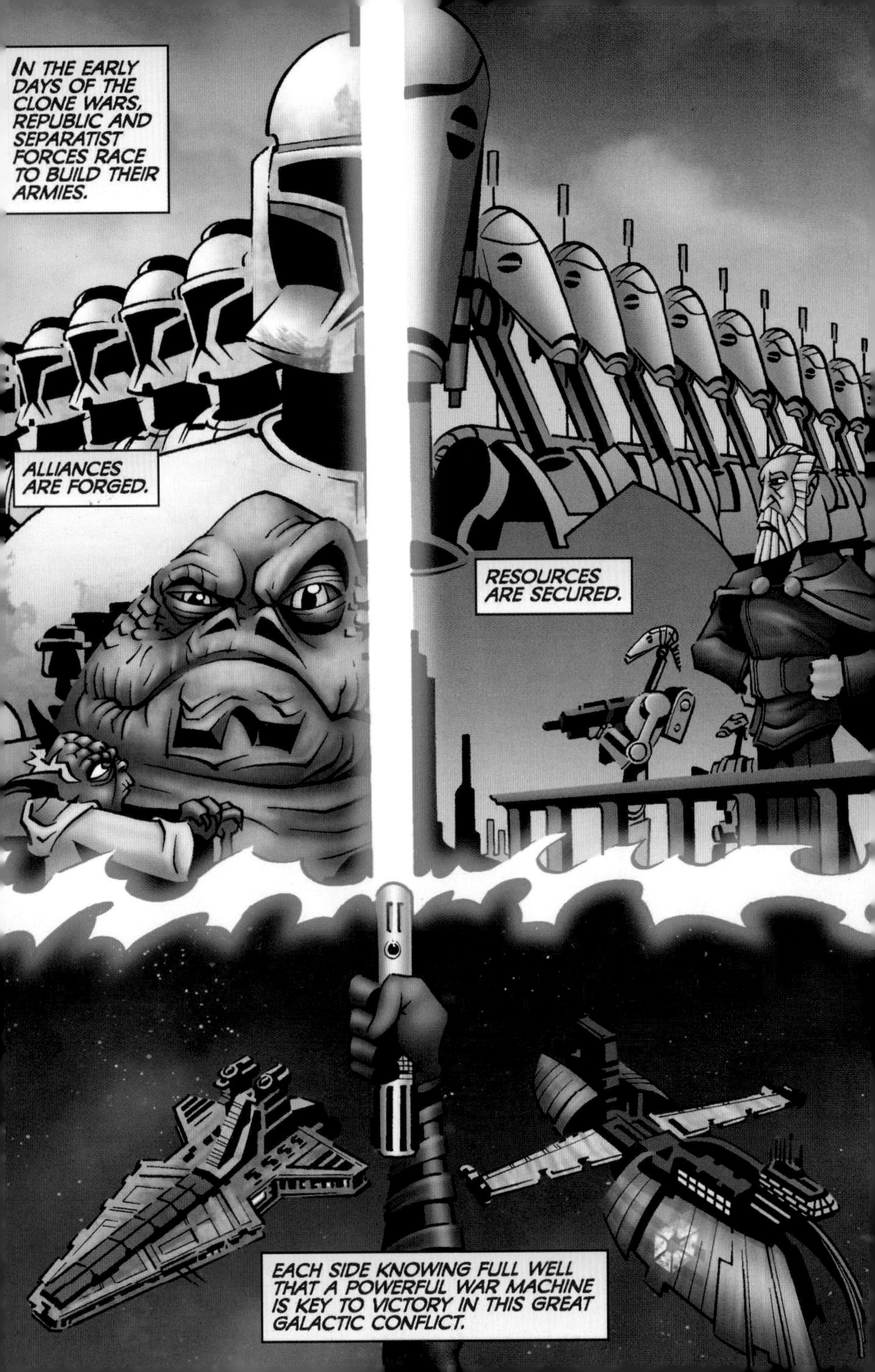
IN THE EARLY DAYS OF THE CLONE WARS, REPUBLIC AND SEPARATIST FORCES RACE TO BUILD THEIR ARMIES.
ALLIANCES ARE FORGED.
RESOURCES ARE SECURED.
EACH SIDE KNOWING FULL WELL THAT A POWERFUL WAR MACHINE IS KEY TO VICTORY IN THIS GREAT GALACTIC CONFLICT.

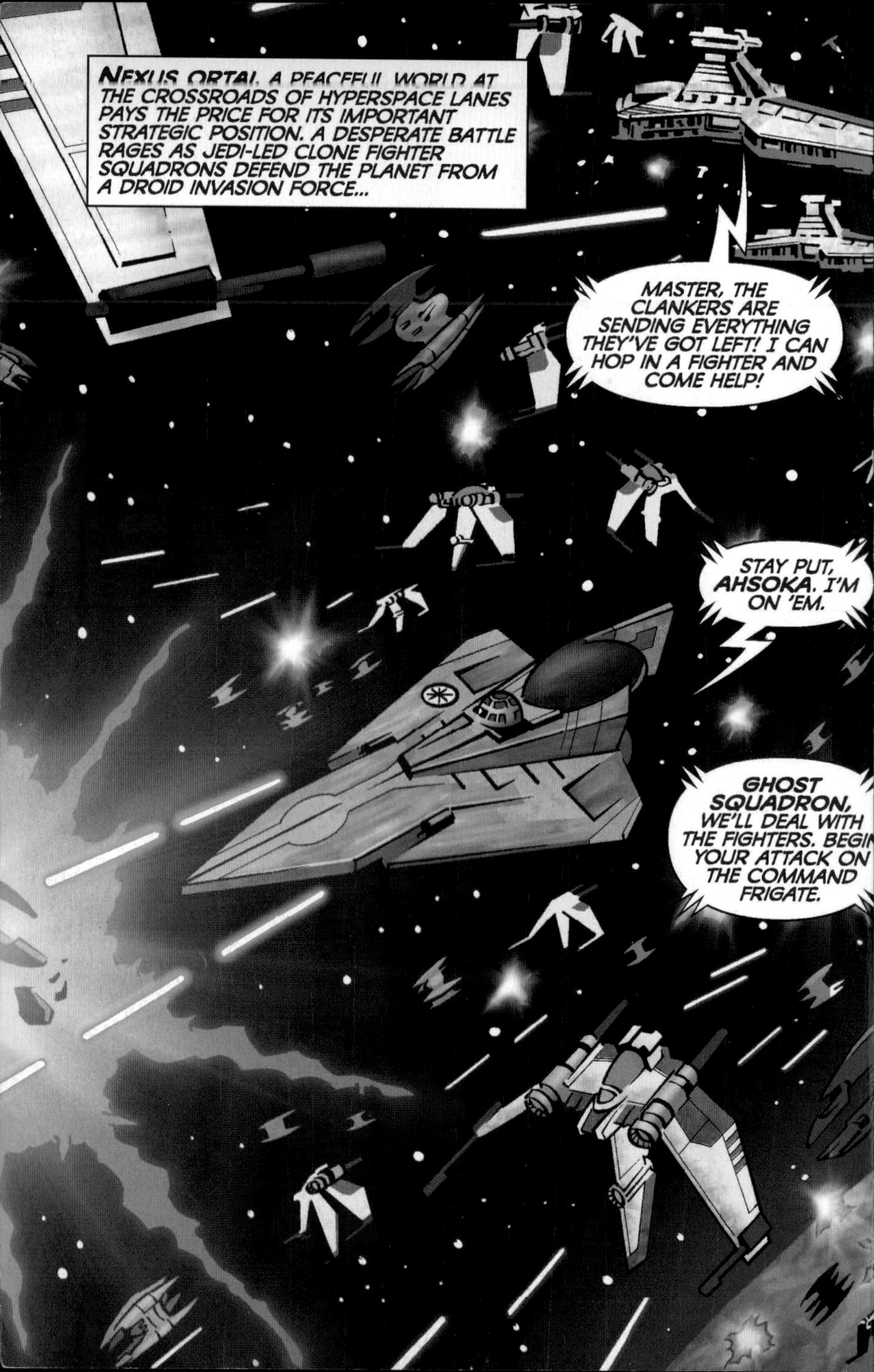
NEXUS ORTAL. A PEACEFUL WORLD AT THE CROSSROADS OF HYPERSPACE LANES PAYS THE PRICE FOR ITS IMPORTANT STRATEGIC POSITION. A DESPERATE BATTLE RAGES AS JEDI-LED CLONE FIGHTER SQUADRONS DEFEND THE PLANET FROM A DROID INVASION FORCE...
MASTER, THE CLANKERS ARE SENDING EVERYTHING THEY'VE GOT LEFT! I CAN HOP IN A FIGHTER AND COME HELP!
STAY PUT, AHSOKA. I'M ON 'EM.
GHOST SQUADRON, WE'LL DEAL WITH THE FIGHTERS. BEGIN YOUR ATTACK ON THE COMMAND FRIGATE.

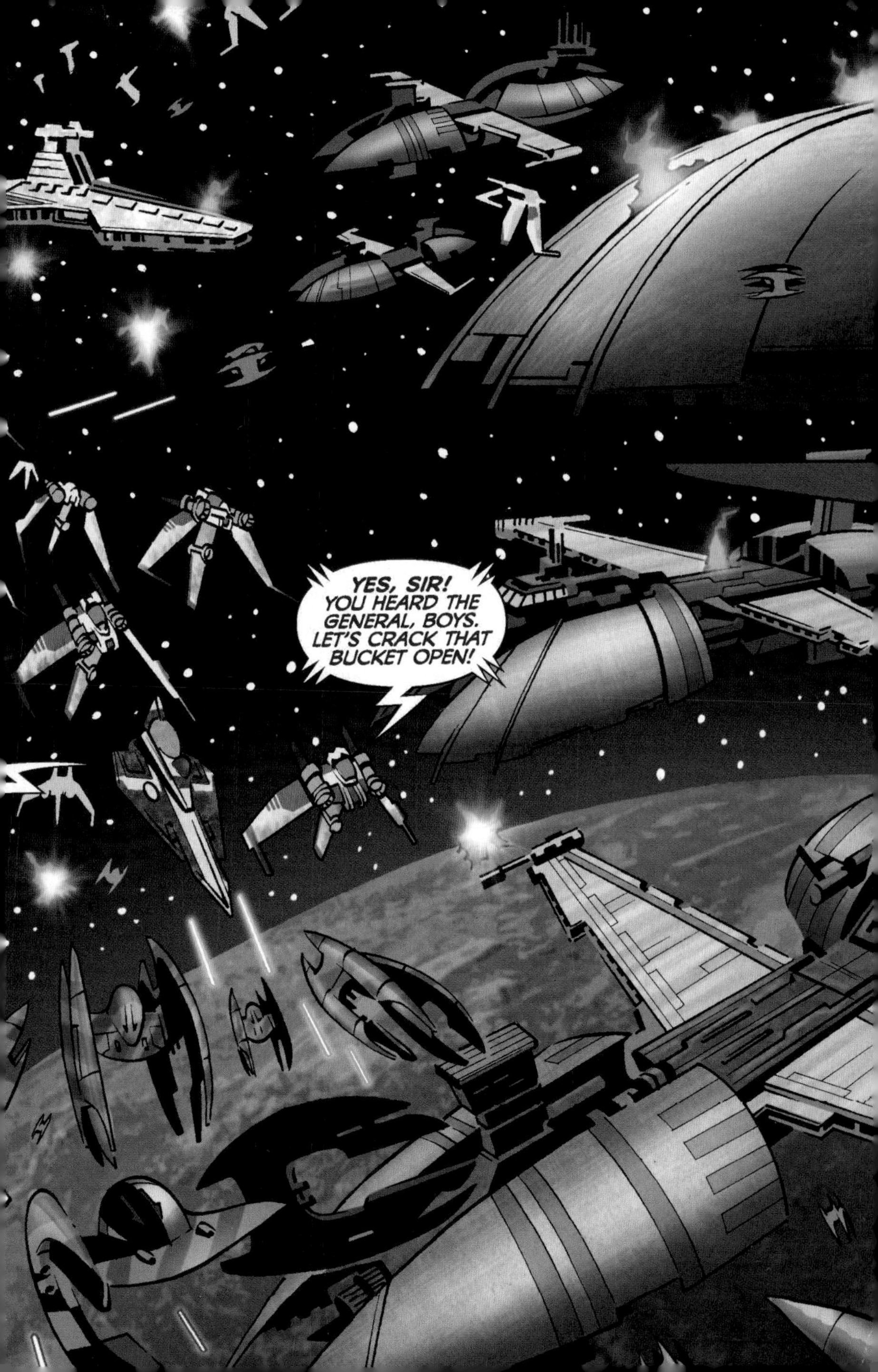
YES, SIR! YOU HEARD THE GENERAL, BOYS. LET'S CRACK THAT BUCKET OPEN!

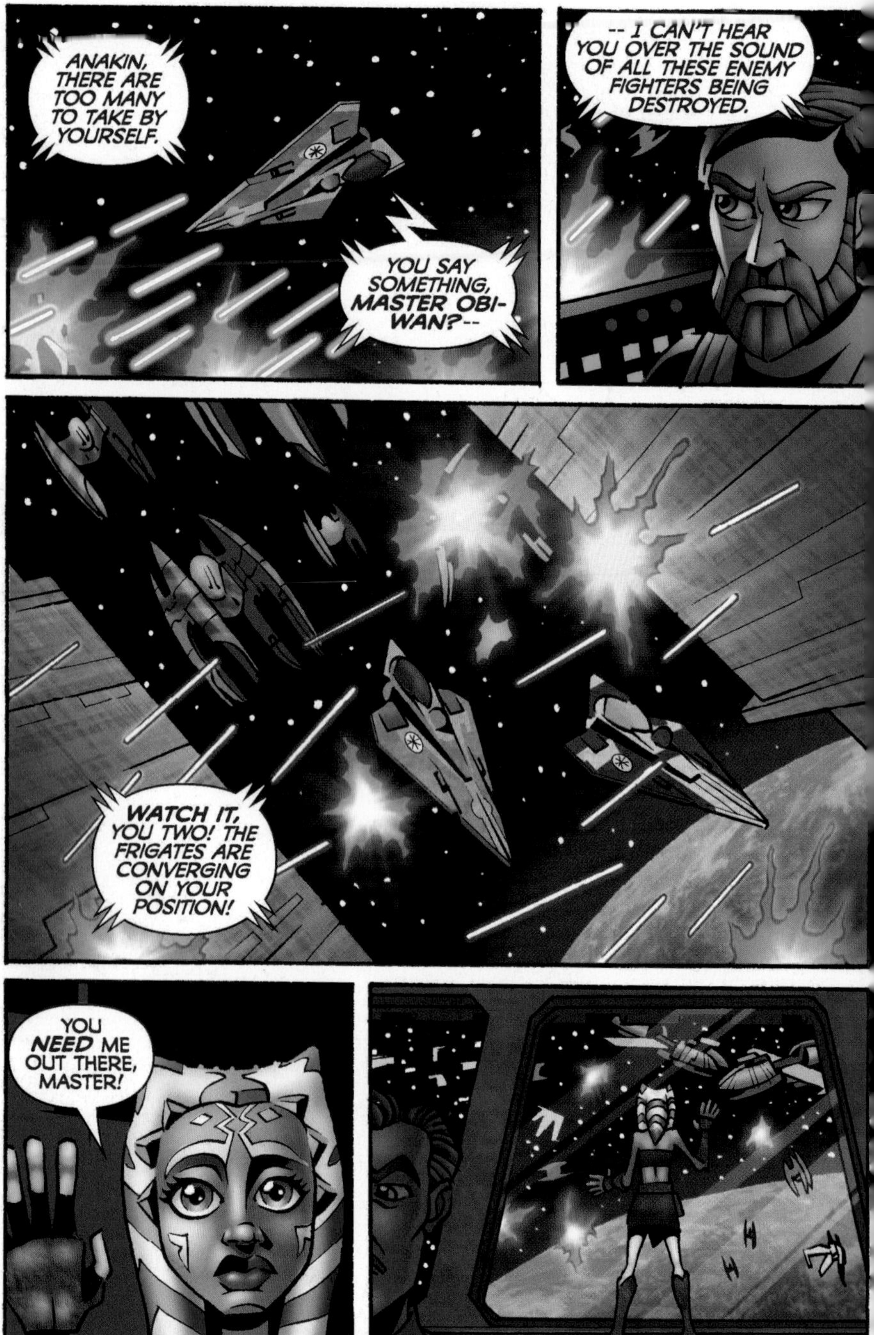
ANAKIN, THERE ARE TOO MANY TO TAKE BY YOURSELF.
YOU SAY SOMETHING, MASTER OBI-WAN?--
-- I CAN'T HEAR YOU OVER THE SOUND OF ALL THESE ENEMY FIGHTERS BEING DESTROYED.
WATCH IT, YOU TWO! THE FRIGATES ARE CONVERGING ON YOUR POSITION!
YOU NEED ME OUT THERE, MASTER!

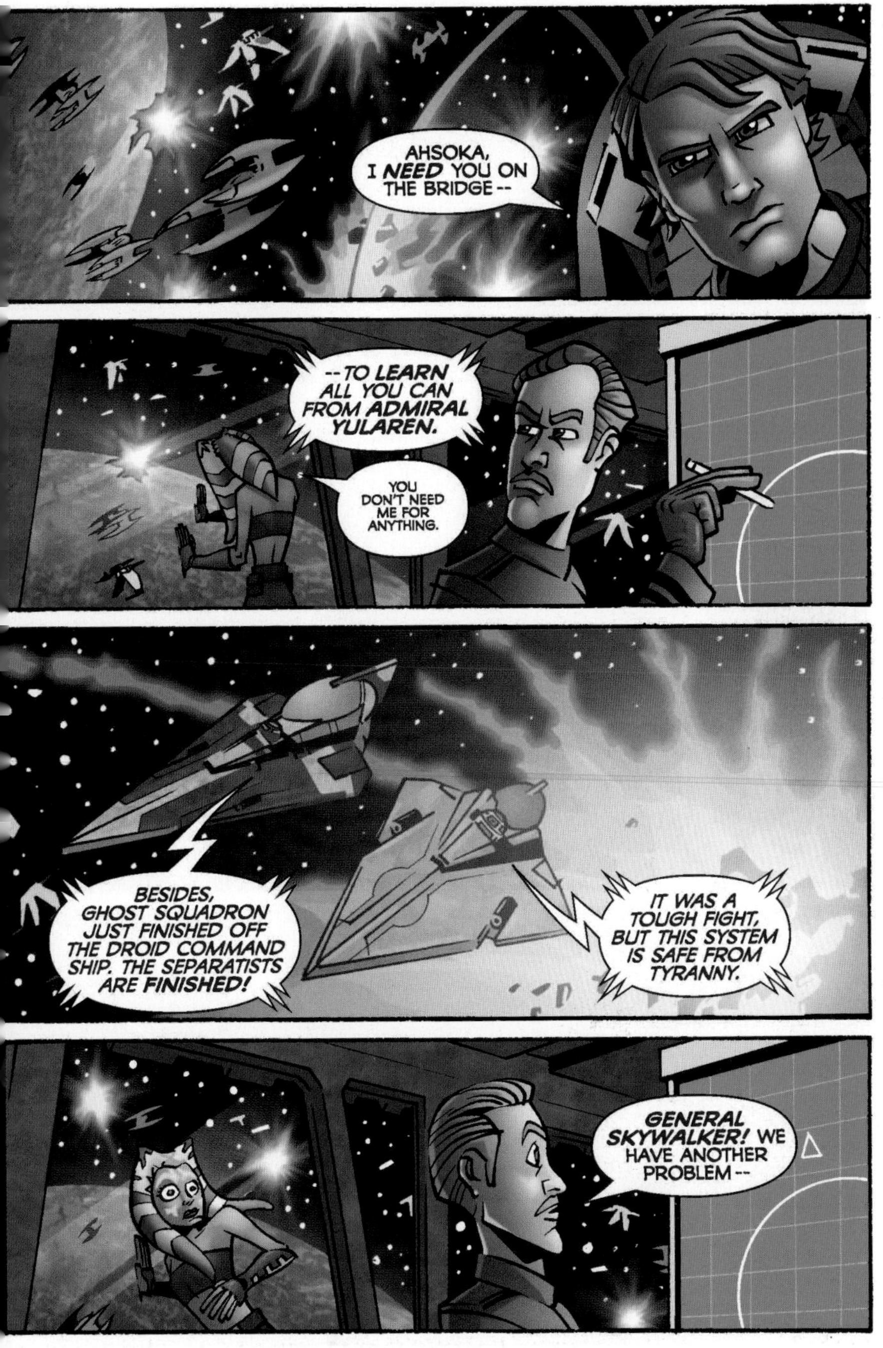
AHSOKA, I NEED YOU ON THE BRIDGE --
--TO LEARN ALL YOU CAN FROM ADMIRAL YULAREN.
YOU DON'T NEED ME FOR ANYTHING.
BESIDES, GHOST SQUADRON JUST FINISHED OFF THE DROID COMMAND SHIP. THE SEPARATISTS ARE FINISHED!
IT WAS A TOUGH FIGHT, BUT THIS SYSTEM IS SAFE FROM TYRANNY.
GENERAL SKYWALKER! WE HAVE ANOTHER PROBLEM --

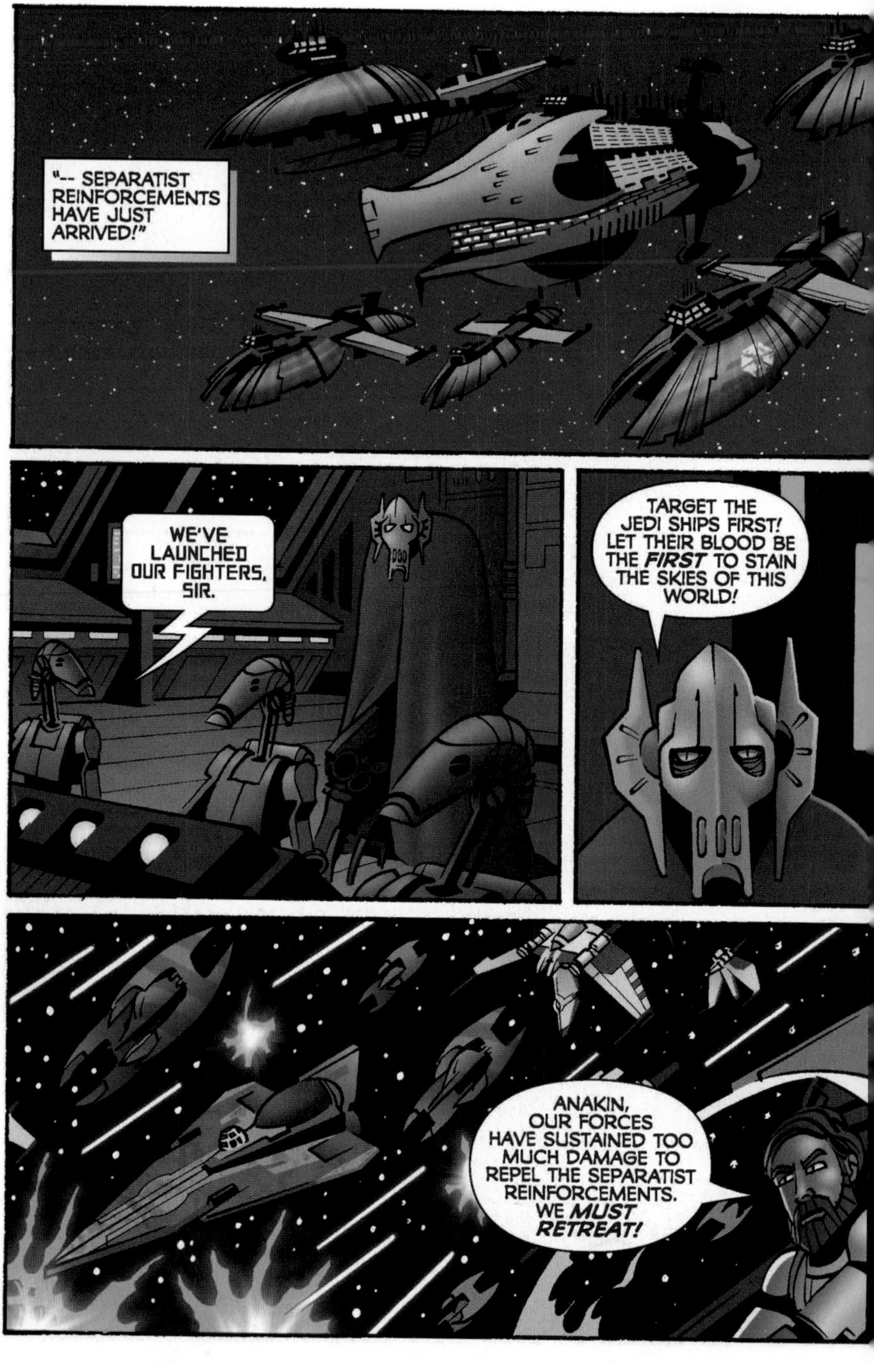
"-- SEPARATIST REINFORCEMENTS HAVE JUST ARRIVED!"
WE'VE LAUNCHED OUR FIGHTERS, SIR.
TARGET THE JEDI SHIPS FIRST! LET THEIR BLOOD BE THE *FIRST* TO STAIN THE SKIES OF THIS WORLD!
ANAKIN, OUR FORCES HAVE SUSTAINED TOO MUCH DAMAGE TO REPEL THE SEPARATIST REINFORCEMENTS. WE *MUST RETREAT!*

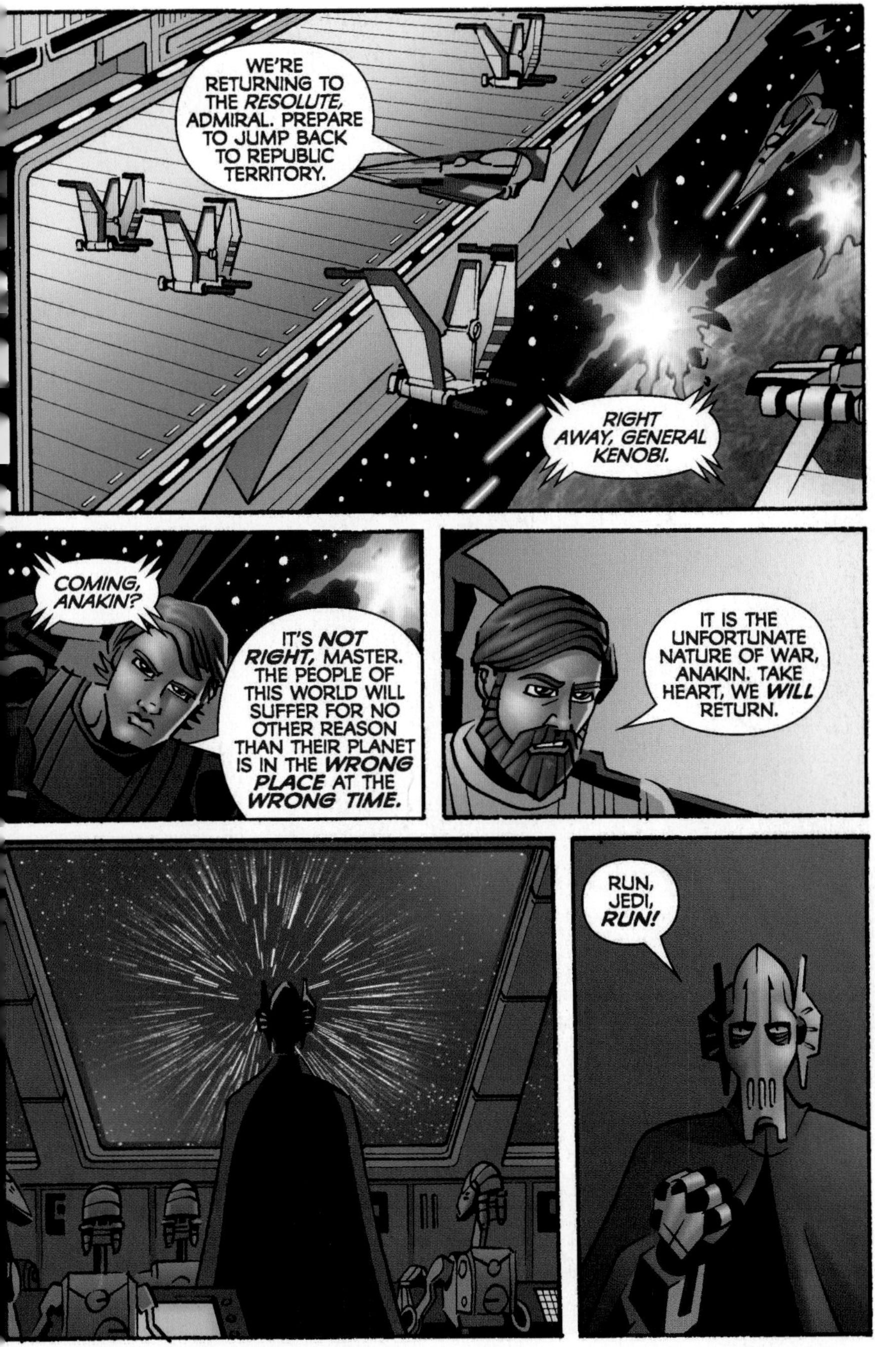
WE'RE RETURNING TO THE *RESOLUTE,* ADMIRAL. PREPARE TO JUMP BACK TO REPUBLIC TERRITORY.
RIGHT AWAY, GENERAL KENOBI.
COMING, ANAKIN?
IT'S ***NOT RIGHT,*** MASTER. THE PEOPLE OF THIS WORLD WILL SUFFER FOR NO OTHER REASON THAN THEIR PLANET IS IN THE ***WRONG PLACE*** AT THE ***WRONG TIME.***
IT IS THE UNFORTUNATE NATURE OF WAR, ANAKIN. TAKE HEART, WE ***WILL*** RETURN.
RUN, JEDI, ***RUN!***

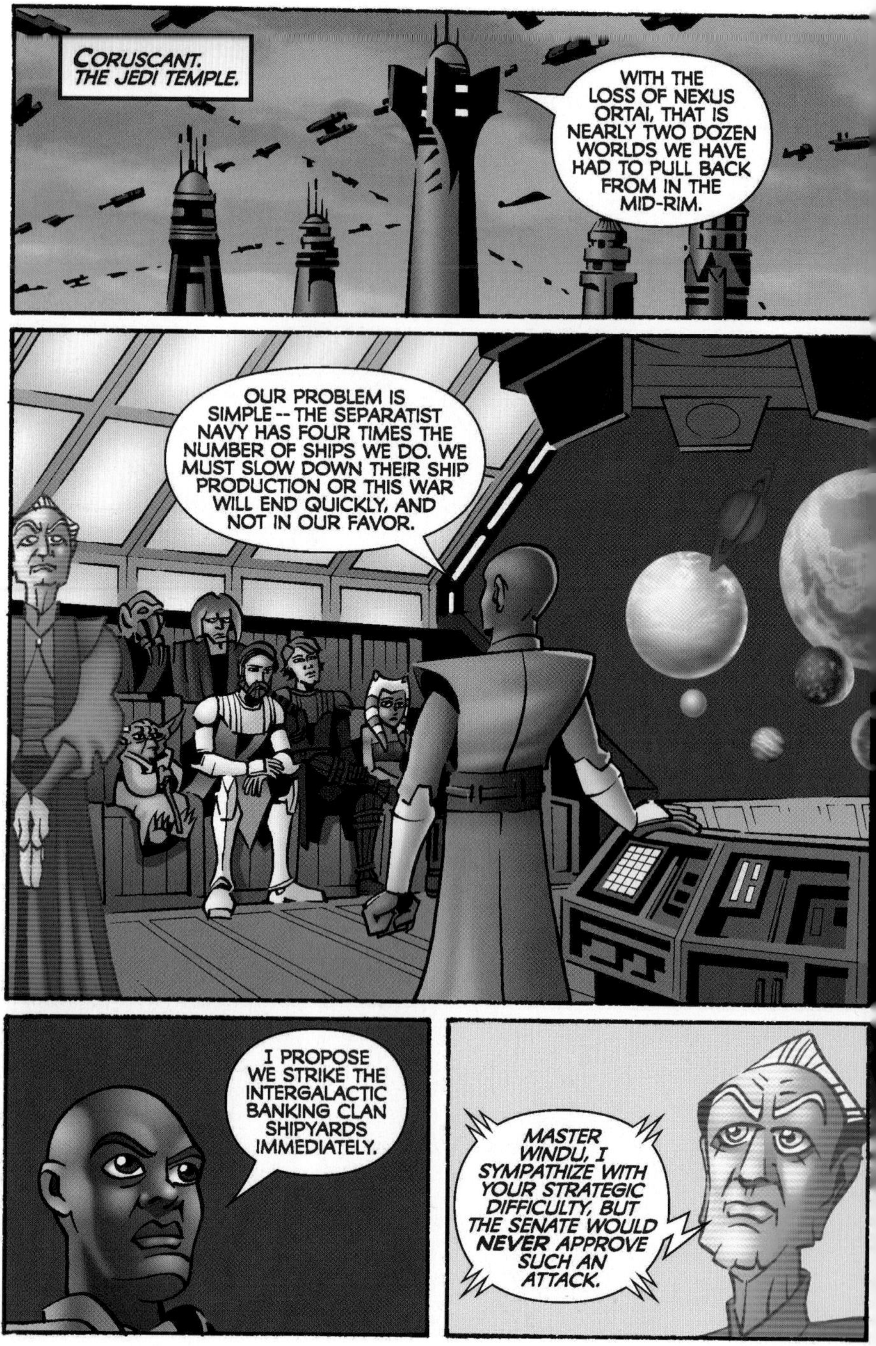
CORUSCANT. THE JEDI TEMPLE.
WITH THE LOSS OF NEXUS ORTAI, THAT IS NEARLY TWO DOZEN WORLDS WE HAVE HAD TO PULL BACK FROM IN THE MID-RIM.
OUR PROBLEM IS SIMPLE -- THE SEPARATIST NAVY HAS FOUR TIMES THE NUMBER OF SHIPS WE DO. WE MUST SLOW DOWN THEIR SHIP PRODUCTION OR THIS WAR WILL END QUICKLY, AND NOT IN OUR FAVOR.
I PROPOSE WE STRIKE THE INTERGALACTIC BANKING CLAN SHIPYARDS IMMEDIATELY.
MASTER WINDU, I SYMPATHIZE WITH YOUR STRATEGIC DIFFICULTY, BUT THE SENATE WOULD NEVER APPROVE SUCH AN ATTACK.

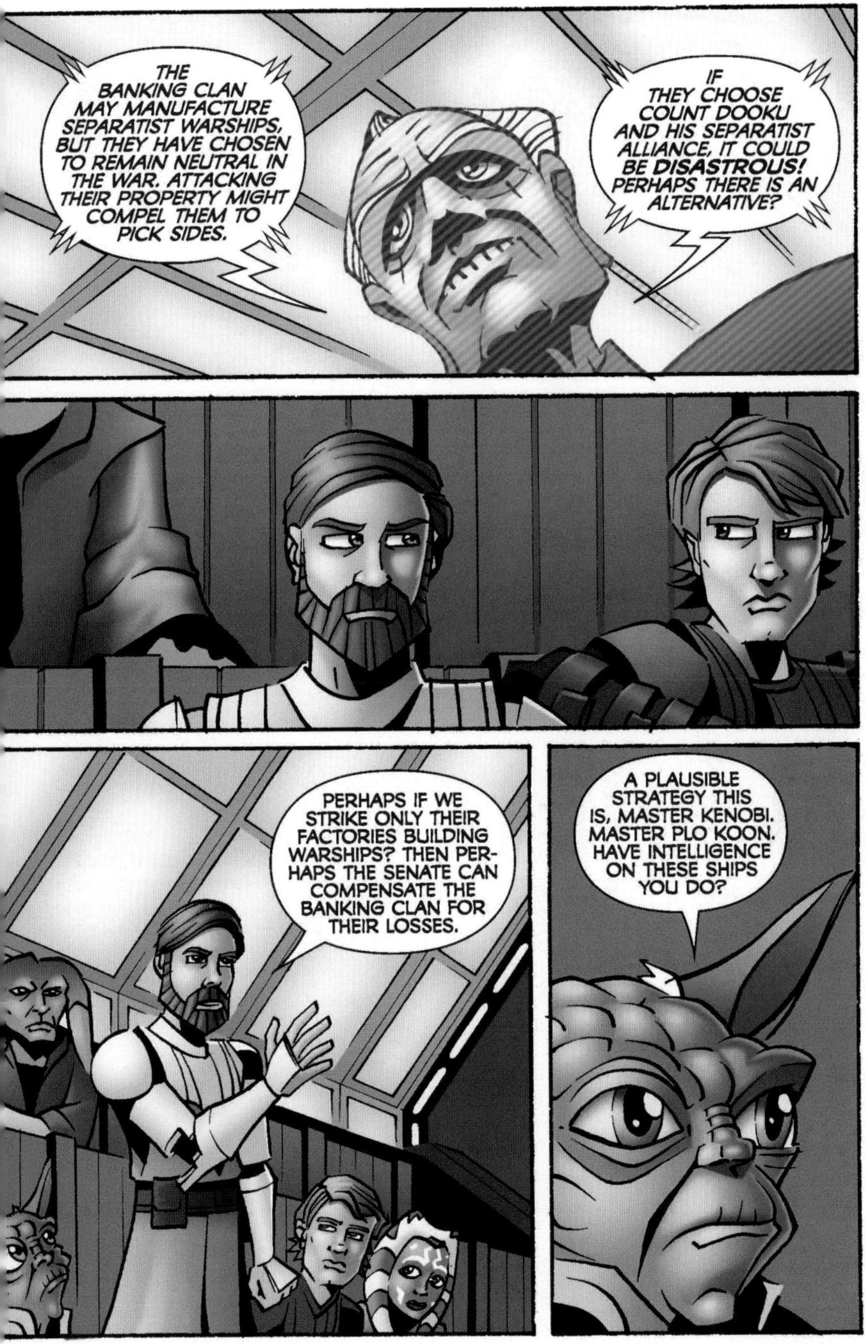
THE BANKING CLAN MAY MANUFACTURE SEPARATIST WARSHIPS, BUT THEY HAVE CHOSEN TO REMAIN NEUTRAL IN THE WAR. ATTACKING THEIR PROPERTY MIGHT COMPEL THEM TO PICK SIDES.
IF THEY CHOOSE COUNT DOOKU AND HIS SEPARATIST ALLIANCE, IT COULD BE **DISASTROUS!** PERHAPS THERE IS AN ALTERNATIVE?
PERHAPS IF WE STRIKE ONLY THEIR FACTORIES BUILDING WARSHIPS? THEN PERHAPS THE SENATE CAN COMPENSATE THE BANKING CLAN FOR THEIR LOSSES.
A PLAUSIBLE STRATEGY THIS IS, MASTER KENOBI. MASTER PLO KOON. HAVE INTELLIGENCE ON THESE SHIPS YOU DO?

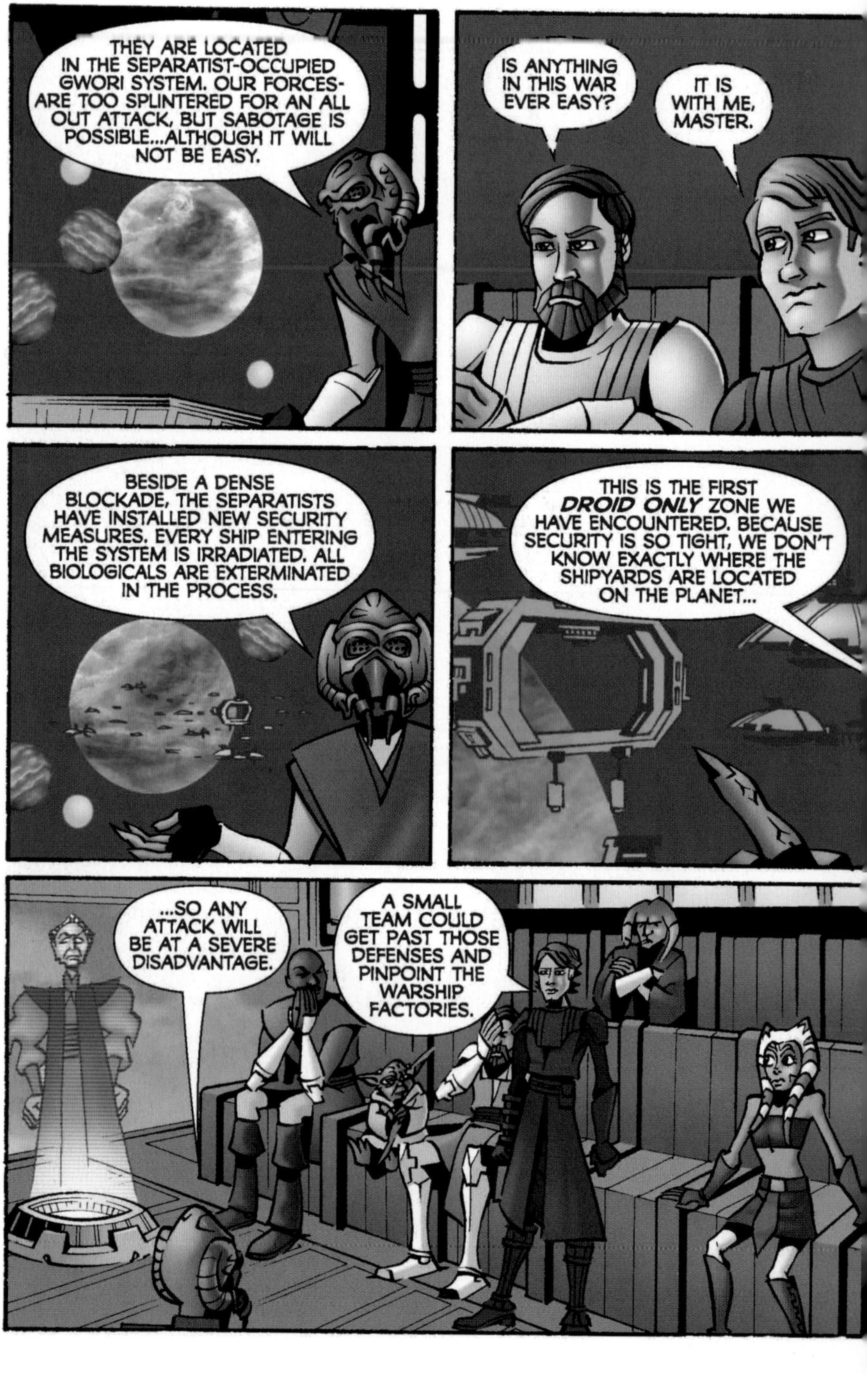
THEY ARE LOCATED IN THE SEPARATIST-OCCUPIED GWORI SYSTEM. OUR FORCES-ARE TOO SPLINTERED FOR AN ALL OUT ATTACK, BUT SABOTAGE IS POSSIBLE...ALTHOUGH IT WILL NOT BE EASY.
IS ANYTHING IN THIS WAR EVER EASY?
IT IS WITH ME, MASTER.
BESIDE A DENSE BLOCKADE, THE SEPARATISTS HAVE INSTALLED NEW SECURITY MEASURES. EVERY SHIP ENTERING THE SYSTEM IS IRRADIATED. ALL BIOLOGICALS ARE EXTERMINATED IN THE PROCESS.
THIS IS THE FIRST DROID ONLY ZONE WE HAVE ENCOUNTERED. BECAUSE SECURITY IS SO TIGHT, WE DON'T KNOW EXACTLY WHERE THE SHIPYARDS ARE LOCATED ON THE PLANET...
...SO ANY ATTACK WILL BE AT A SEVERE DISADVANTAGE.
A SMALL TEAM COULD GET PAST THOSE DEFENSES AND PINPOINT THE WARSHIP FACTORIES.

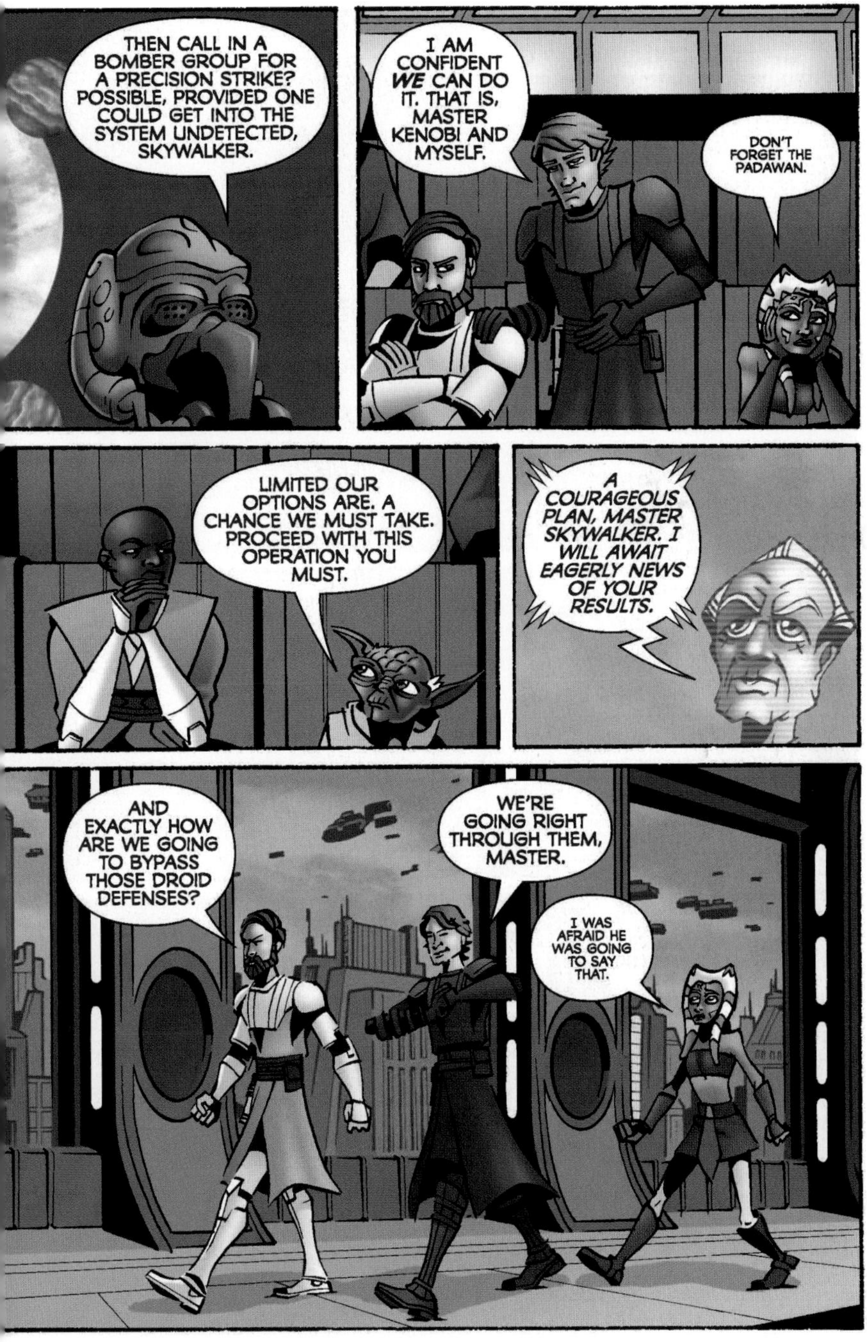

THEN CALL IN A BOMBER GROUP FOR A PRECISION STRIKE? POSSIBLE, PROVIDED ONE COULD GET INTO THE SYSTEM UNDETECTED, SKYWALKER.
I AM CONFIDENT *WE* CAN DO IT. THAT IS, MASTER KENOBI AND MYSELF.
DON'T FORGET THE PADAWAN.
LIMITED OUR OPTIONS ARE. A CHANCE WE MUST TAKE. PROCEED WITH THIS OPERATION YOU MUST.
A COURAGEOUS PLAN, MASTER SKYWALKER. I WILL AWAIT EAGERLY NEWS OF YOUR RESULTS.
AND EXACTLY HOW ARE WE GOING TO BYPASS THOSE DROID DEFENSES?
WE'RE GOING RIGHT THROUGH THEM, MASTER.
I WAS AFRAID HE WAS GOING TO SAY THAT.

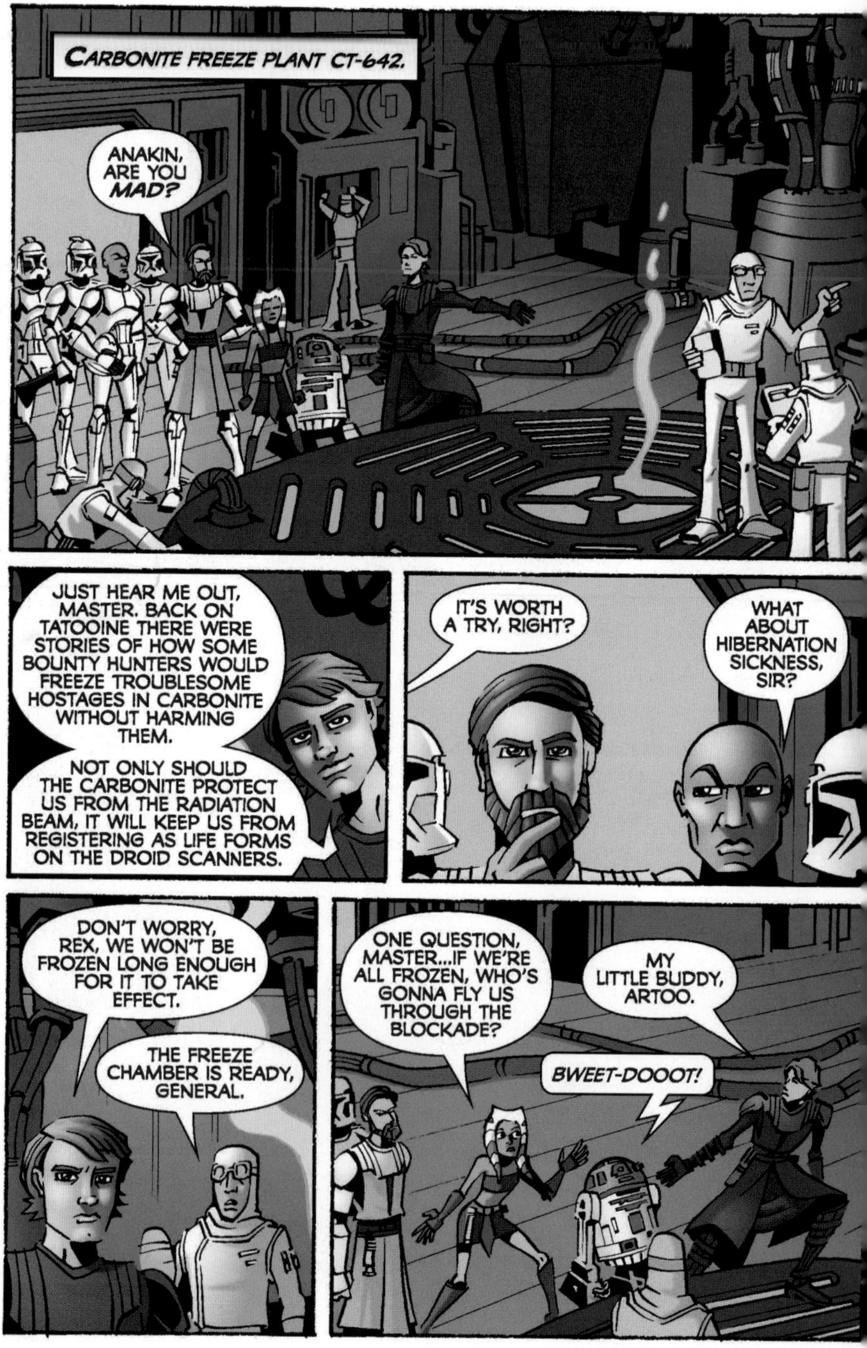
CARBONITE FREEZE PLANT CT-642.
ANAKIN, ARE YOU MAD?
JUST HEAR ME OUT, MASTER. BACK ON TATOOINE THERE WERE STORIES OF HOW SOME BOUNTY HUNTERS WOULD FREEZE TROUBLESOME HOSTAGES IN CARBONITE WITHOUT HARMING THEM.
NOT ONLY SHOULD THE CARBONITE PROTECT US FROM THE RADIATION BEAM, IT WILL KEEP US FROM REGISTERING AS LIFE FORMS ON THE DROID SCANNERS.
IT'S WORTH A TRY, RIGHT?
WHAT ABOUT HIBERNATION SICKNESS, SIR?
DON'T WORRY, REX, WE WON'T BE FROZEN LONG ENOUGH FOR IT TO TAKE EFFECT.
THE FREEZE CHAMBER IS READY, GENERAL.
ONE QUESTION, MASTER...IF WE'RE ALL FROZEN, WHO'S GONNA FLY US THROUGH THE BLOCKADE?
MY LITTLE BUDDY, ARTOO.
BWEET-DOOOT!

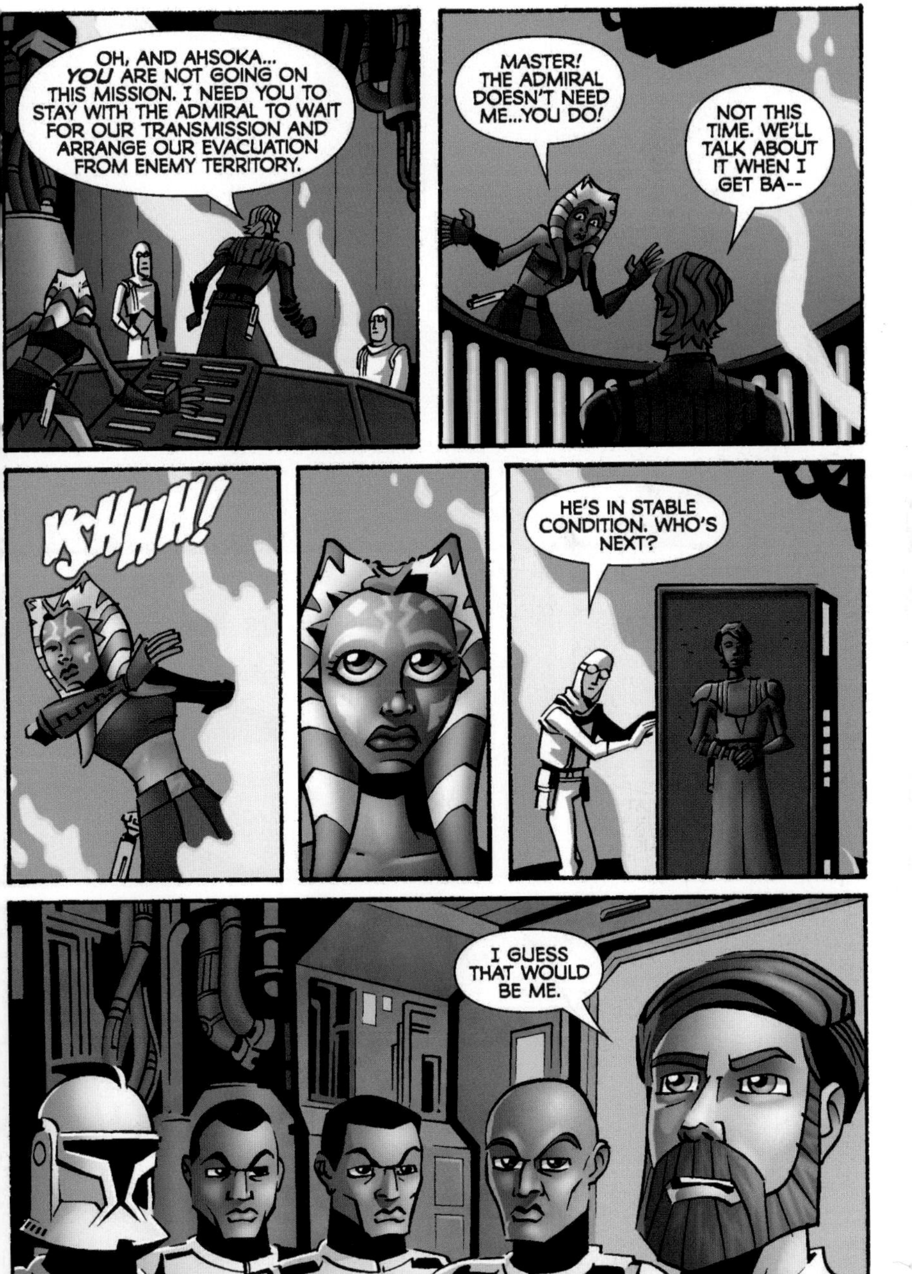
OH, AND AHSOKA... *YOU* ARE NOT GOING ON THIS MISSION. I NEED YOU TO STAY WITH THE ADMIRAL TO WAIT FOR OUR TRANSMISSION AND ARRANGE OUR EVACUATION FROM ENEMY TERRITORY.
MASTER! THE ADMIRAL DOESN'T NEED ME...YOU DO!
NOT THIS TIME. WE'LL TALK ABOUT IT WHEN I GET BA--
KSHHH!
HE'S IN STABLE CONDITION. WHO'S NEXT?
I GUESS THAT WOULD BE ME.

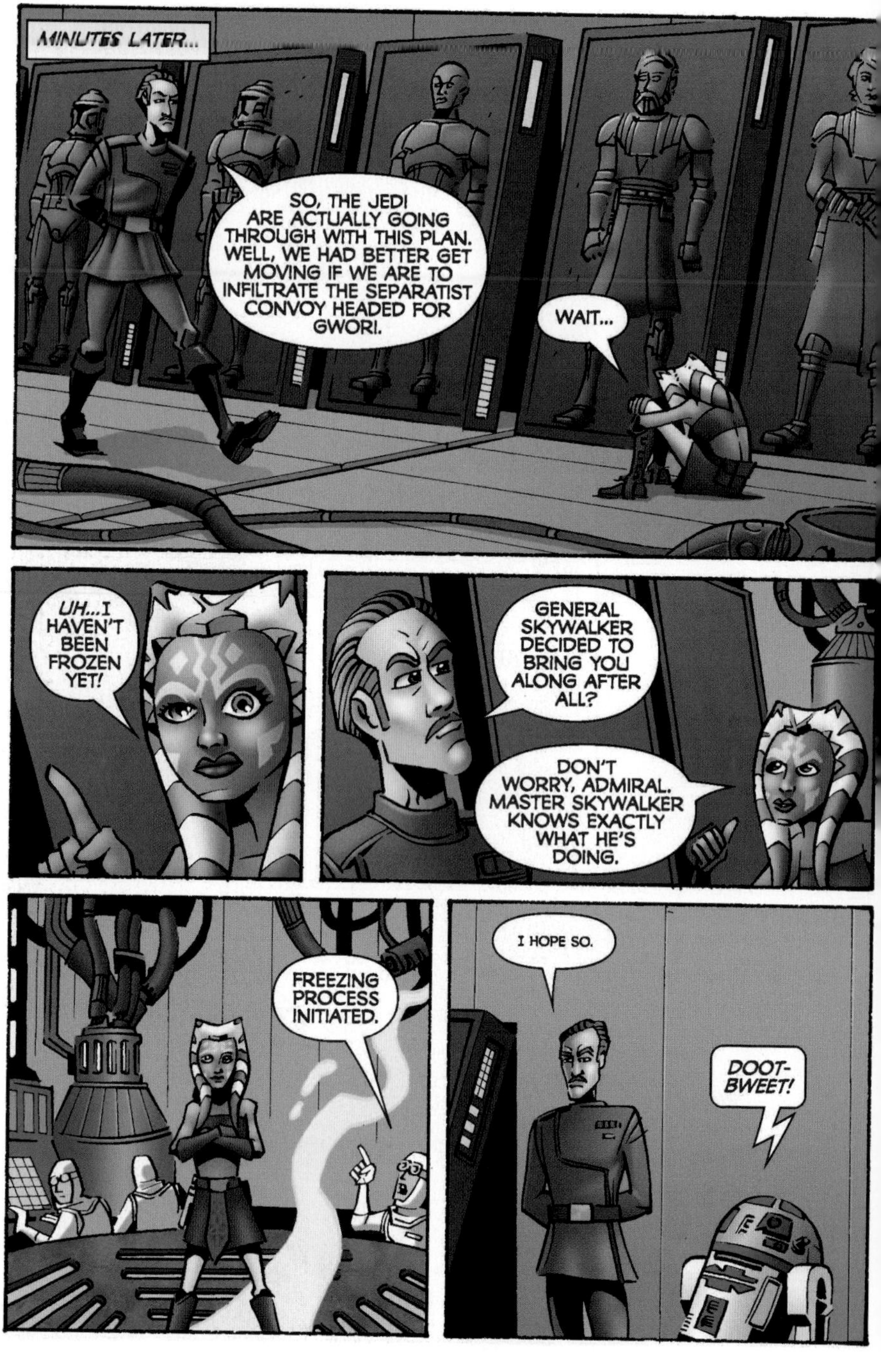
MINUTES LATER...
SO, THE JEDI ARE ACTUALLY GOING THROUGH WITH THIS PLAN. WELL, WE HAD BETTER GET MOVING IF WE ARE TO INFILTRATE THE SEPARATIST CONVOY HEADED FOR GWORI.
WAIT...
UH...I HAVEN'T BEEN FROZEN YET!
GENERAL SKYWALKER DECIDED TO BRING YOU ALONG AFTER ALL?
DON'T WORRY, ADMIRAL. MASTER SKYWALKER KNOWS EXACTLY WHAT HE'S DOING.
FREEZING PROCESS INITIATED.
I HOPE SO.
DOOT-BWEET!

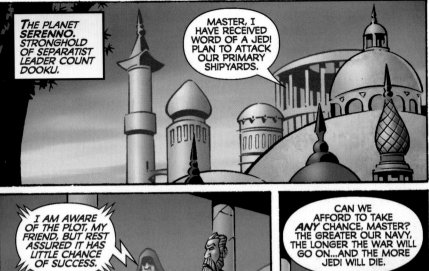

THE PLANET *SERENNO.* STRONGHOLD OF SEPARATIST LEADER COUNT DOOKU.

MASTER, I HAVE RECEIVED WORD OF A JEDI PLAN TO ATTACK OUR PRIMARY SHIPYARDS.

I AM AWARE OF THE PLOT, MY FRIEND, BUT REST ASSURED IT HAS LITTLE CHANCE OF SUCCESS.

CAN WE AFFORD TO TAKE *ANY* CHANCE, MASTER? THE GREATER OUR NAVY, THE LONGER THE WAR WILL GO ON...AND THE MORE JEDI WILL DIE.

WE ARE EARLY IN THIS CONFLICT, LORD TYRANUS. I AM MORE INTERESTED IN LEARNING WHICH OF OUR SEPARATIST PAWNS CAN BE RELIED UPON --

-- AND WHICH JEDI WILL PROVE THEMSELVES AS OUR GREATEST THREATS.

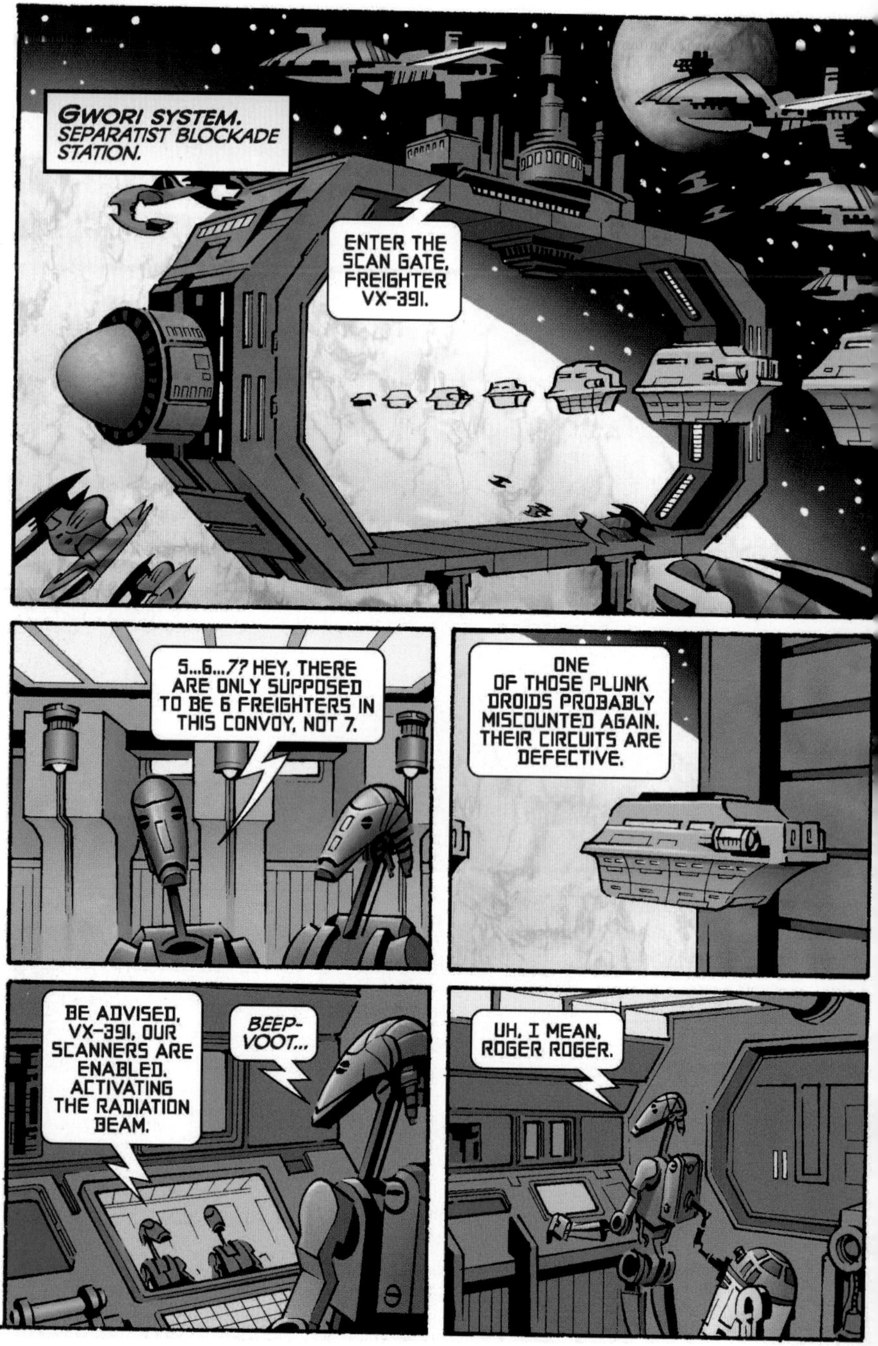
GWORI SYSTEM. SEPARATIST BLOCKADE STATION.
ENTER THE SCAN GATE, FREIGHTER VX-391.
5...6...7? HEY, THERE ARE ONLY SUPPOSED TO BE 6 FREIGHTERS IN THIS CONVOY, NOT 7.
ONE OF THOSE PLUNK DROIDS PROBABLY MISCOUNTED AGAIN. THEIR CIRCUITS ARE DEFECTIVE.
BE ADVISED, VX-391, OUR SCANNERS ARE ENABLED. ACTIVATING THE RADIATION BEAM.
BEEP-VOOT...
UH, I MEAN, ROGER ROGER.

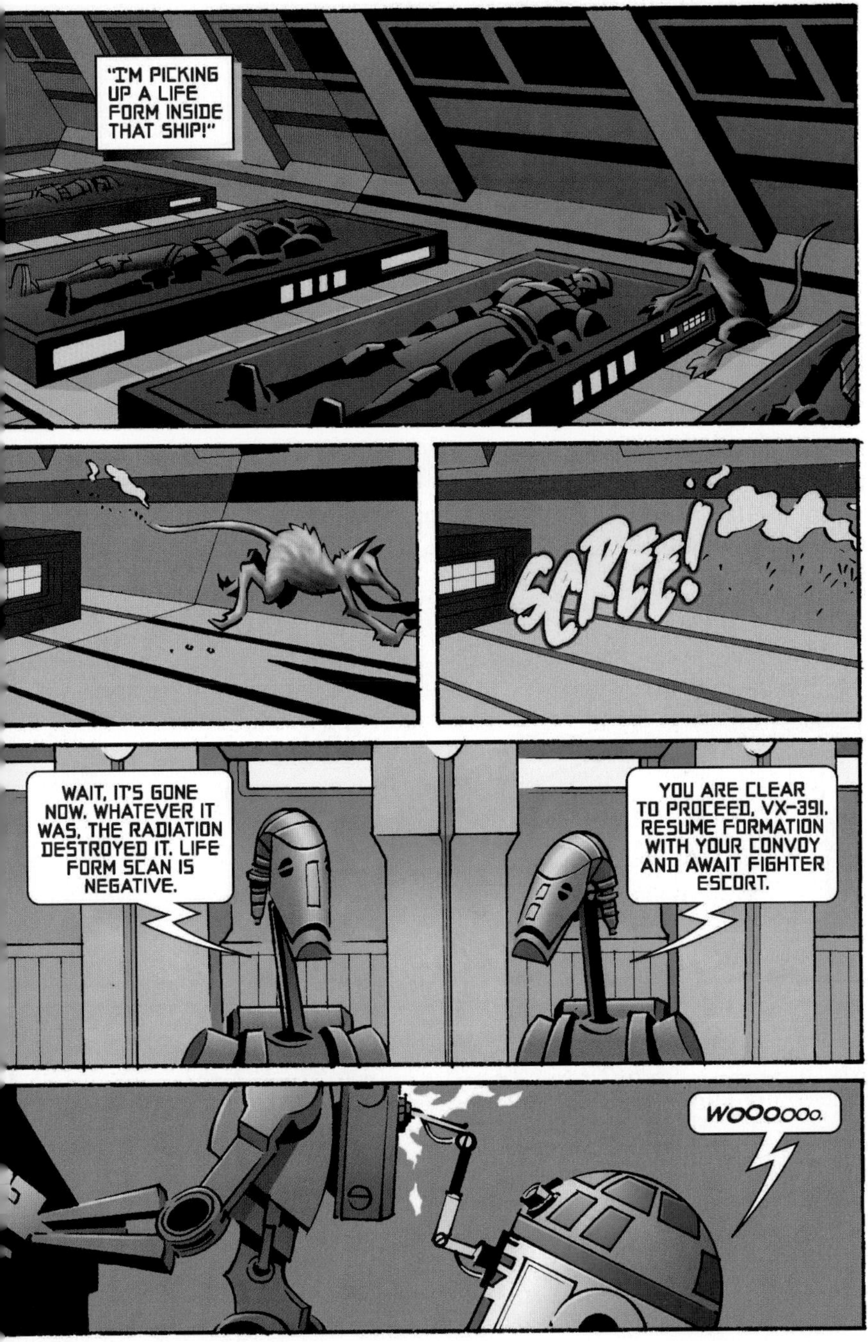
"I'M PICKING UP A LIFE FORM INSIDE THAT SHIP!"
SCREE!
WAIT, IT'S GONE NOW. WHATEVER IT WAS, THE RADIATION DESTROYED IT. LIFE FORM SCAN IS NEGATIVE.
YOU ARE CLEAR TO PROCEED, VX-391. RESUME FORMATION WITH YOUR CONVOY AND AWAIT FIGHTER ESCORT.
WOOOooo.

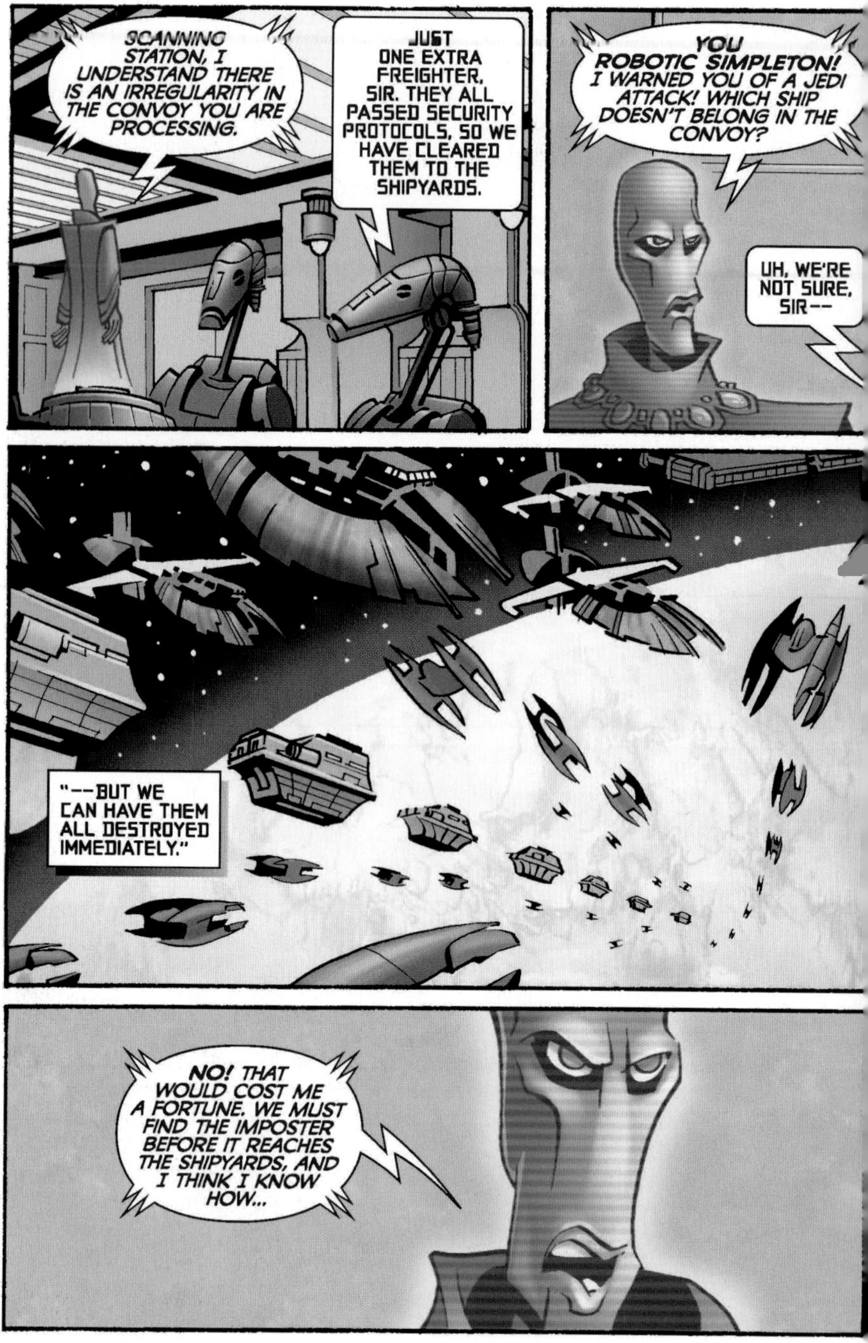
SCANNING STATION, I UNDERSTAND THERE IS AN IRREGULARITY IN THE CONVOY YOU ARE PROCESSING.
JUST ONE EXTRA FREIGHTER, SIR. THEY ALL PASSED SECURITY PROTOCOLS, SO WE HAVE CLEARED THEM TO THE SHIPYARDS.
YOU ROBOTIC SIMPLETON! I WARNED YOU OF A JEDI ATTACK! WHICH SHIP DOESN'T BELONG IN THE CONVOY?
UH, WE'RE NOT SURE, SIR--
"--BUT WE CAN HAVE THEM ALL DESTROYED IMMEDIATELY."
NO! THAT WOULD COST ME A FORTUNE. WE MUST FIND THE IMPOSTER BEFORE IT REACHES THE SHIPYARDS, AND I THINK I KNOW HOW...

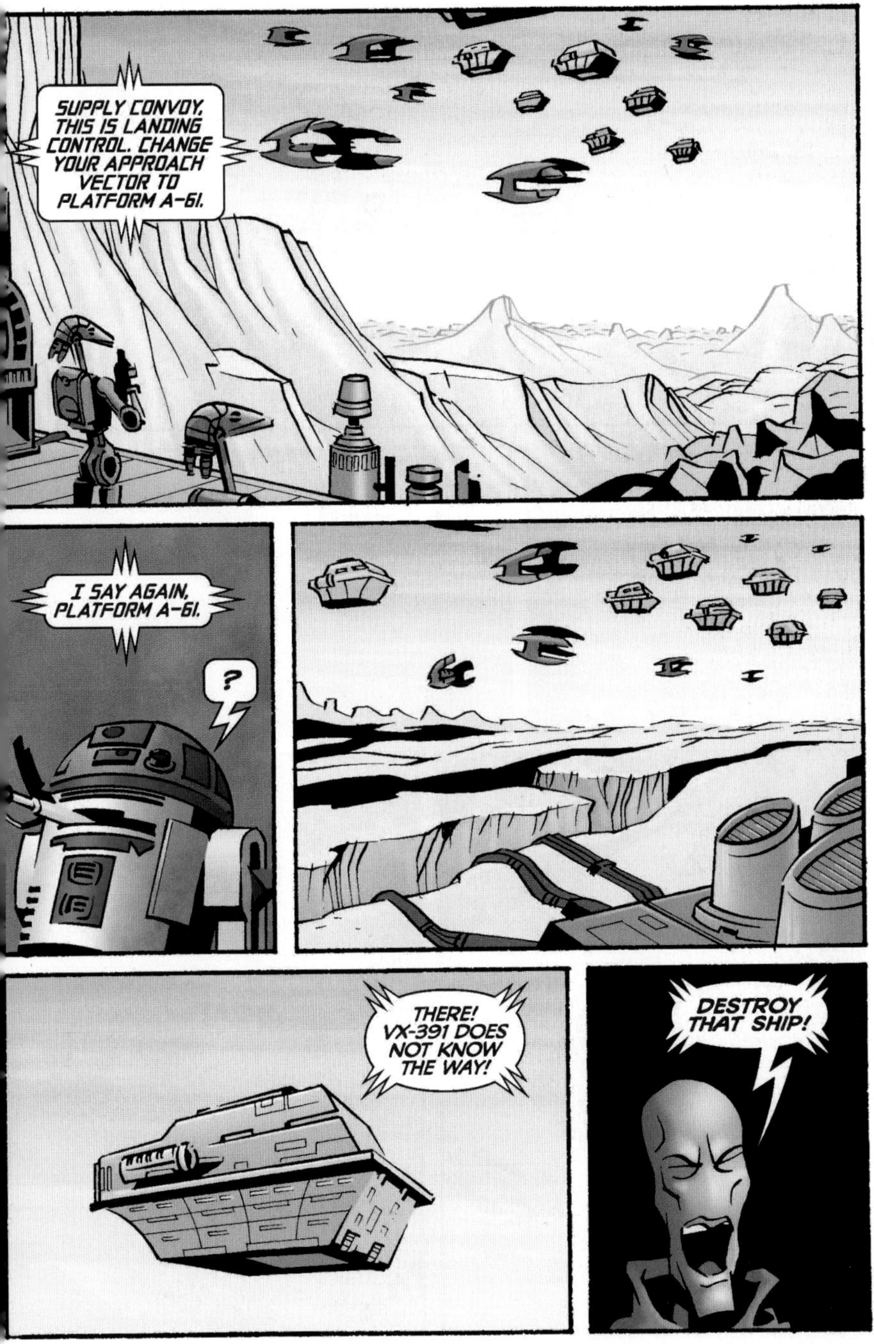
SUPPLY CONVOY, THIS IS LANDING CONTROL. CHANGE YOUR APPROACH VECTOR TO PLATFORM A-61.
I SAY AGAIN, PLATFORM A-61.
?
THERE! VX-391 DOES NOT KNOW THE WAY!
DESTROY THAT SHIP!

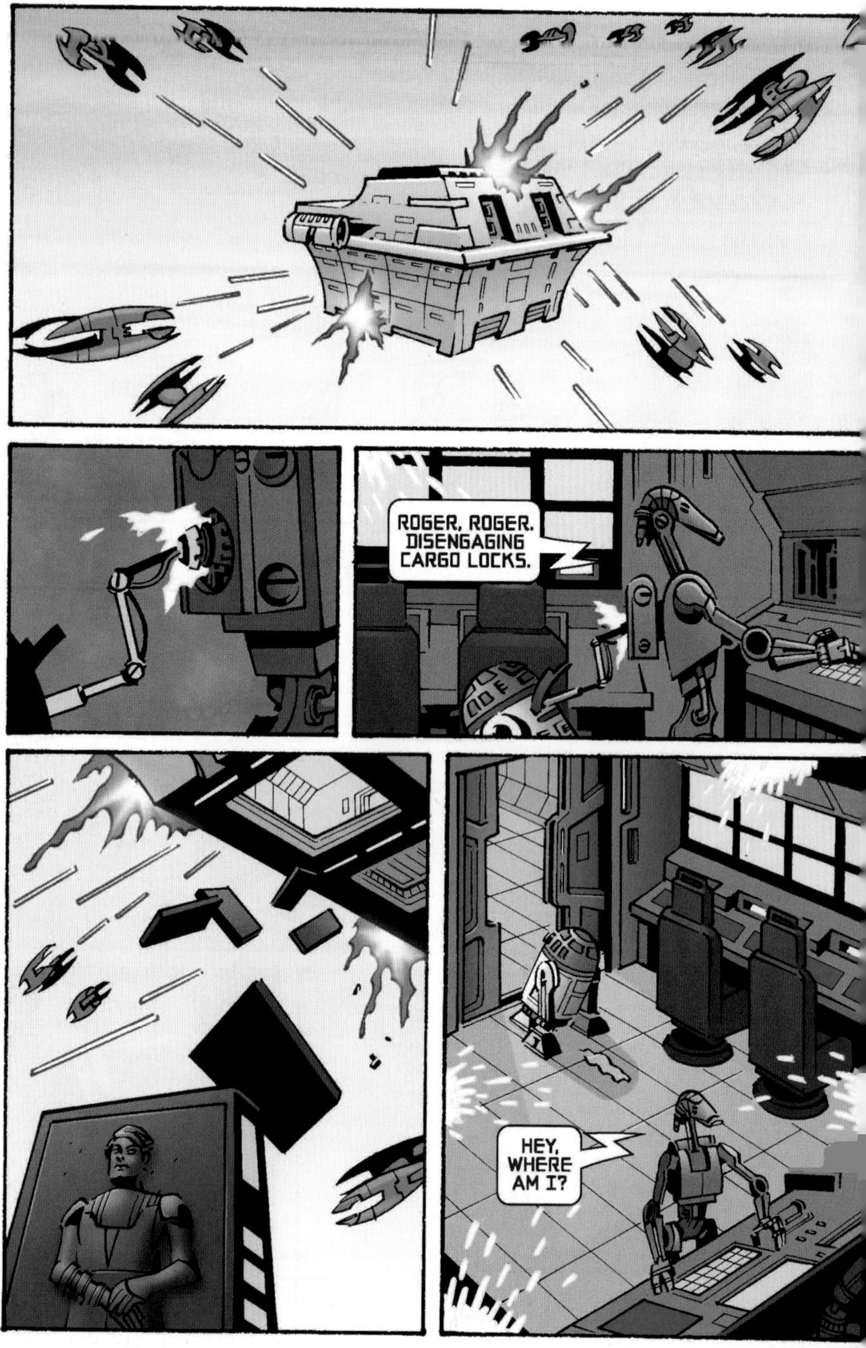
ROGER, ROGER. DISENGAGING CARGO LOCKS.
HEY, WHERE AM I?

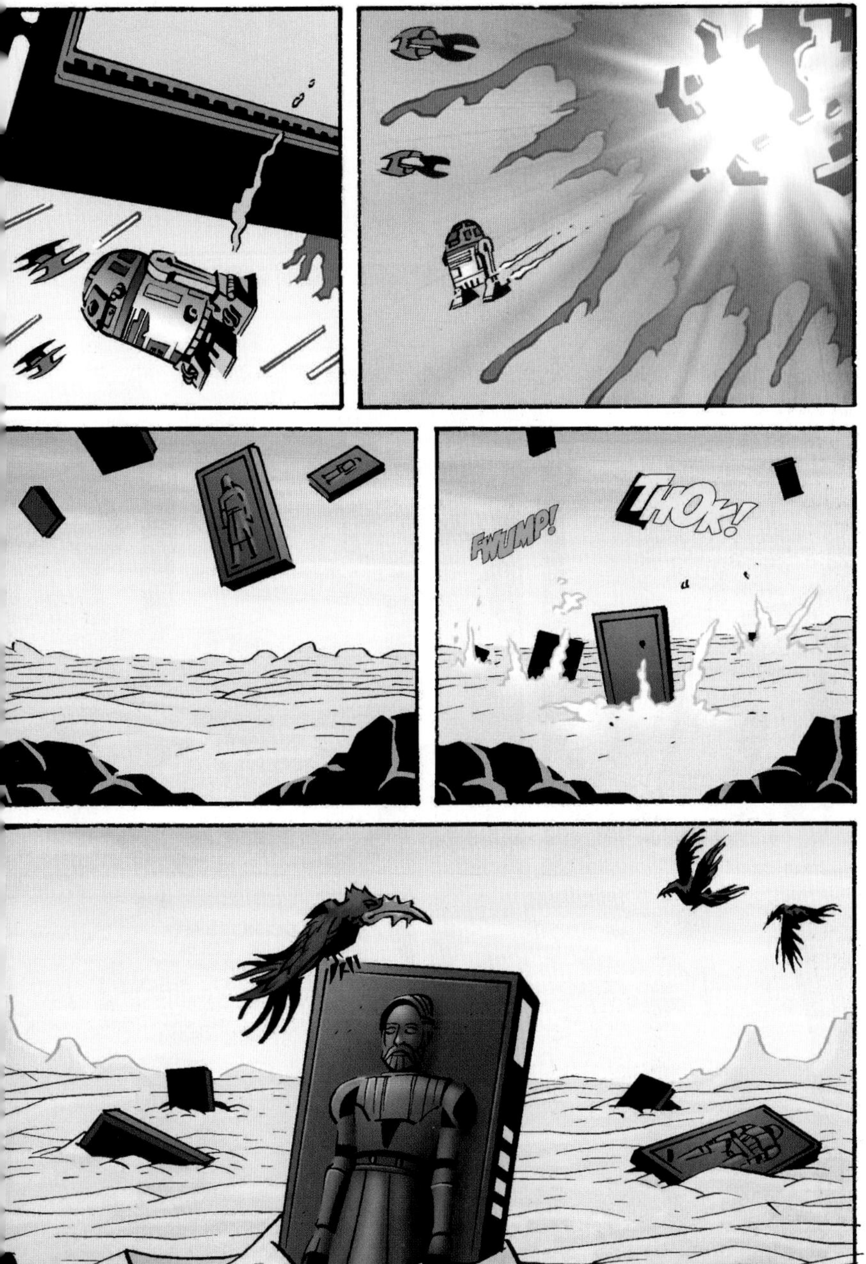
FWUMP!
THOK!

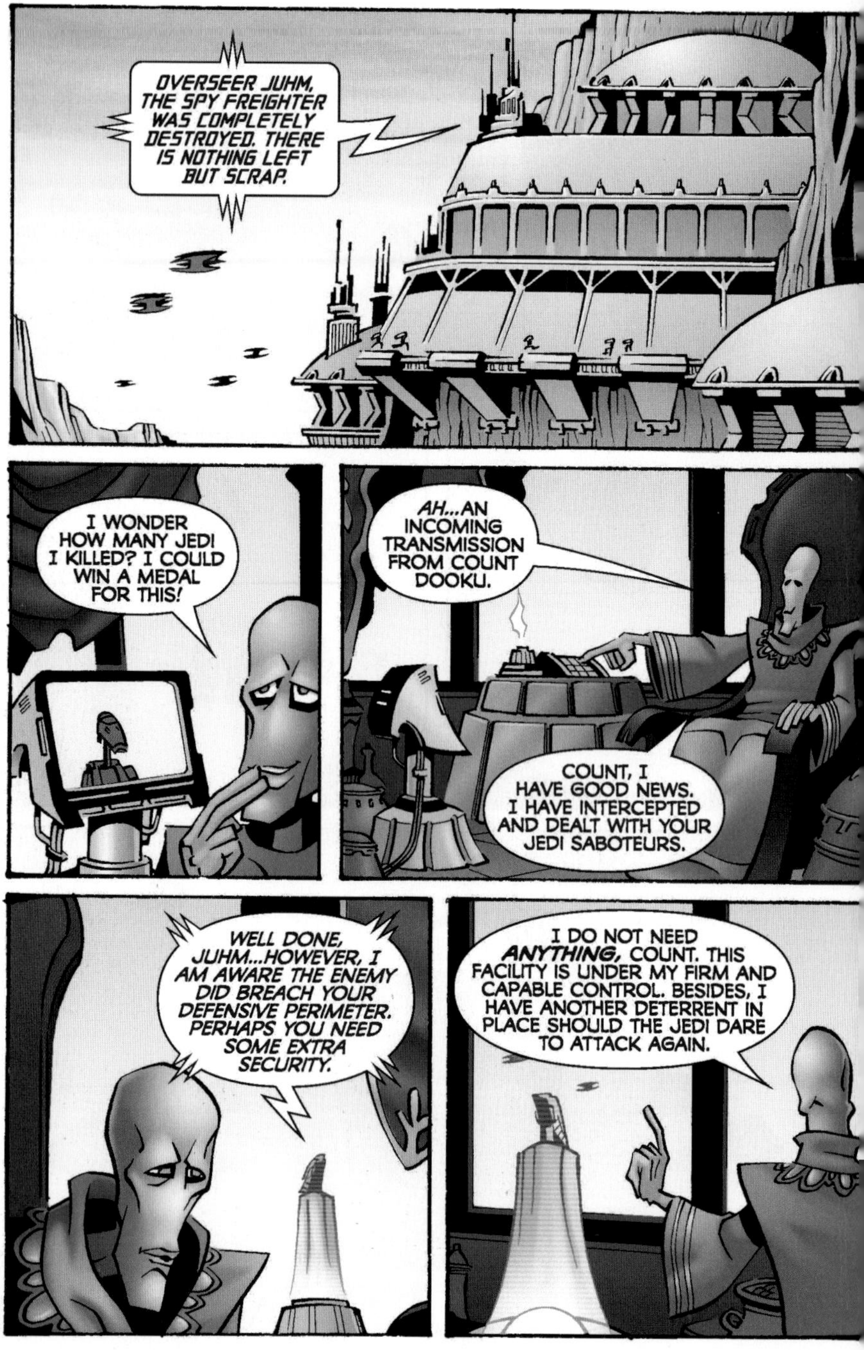
OVERSEER JUHM, THE SPY FREIGHTER WAS COMPLETELY DESTROYED. THERE IS NOTHING LEFT BUT SCRAP.
I WONDER HOW MANY JEDI I KILLED? I COULD WIN A MEDAL FOR THIS!
AH...AN INCOMING TRANSMISSION FROM COUNT DOOKU.
COUNT, I HAVE GOOD NEWS. I HAVE INTERCEPTED AND DEALT WITH YOUR JEDI SABOTEURS.
WELL DONE, JUHM...HOWEVER, I AM AWARE THE ENEMY DID BREACH YOUR DEFENSIVE PERIMETER. PERHAPS YOU NEED SOME EXTRA SECURITY.
I DO NOT NEED ANYTHING, COUNT. THIS FACILITY IS UNDER MY FIRM AND CAPABLE CONTROL. BESIDES, I HAVE ANOTHER DETERRENT IN PLACE SHOULD THE JEDI DARE TO ATTACK AGAIN.

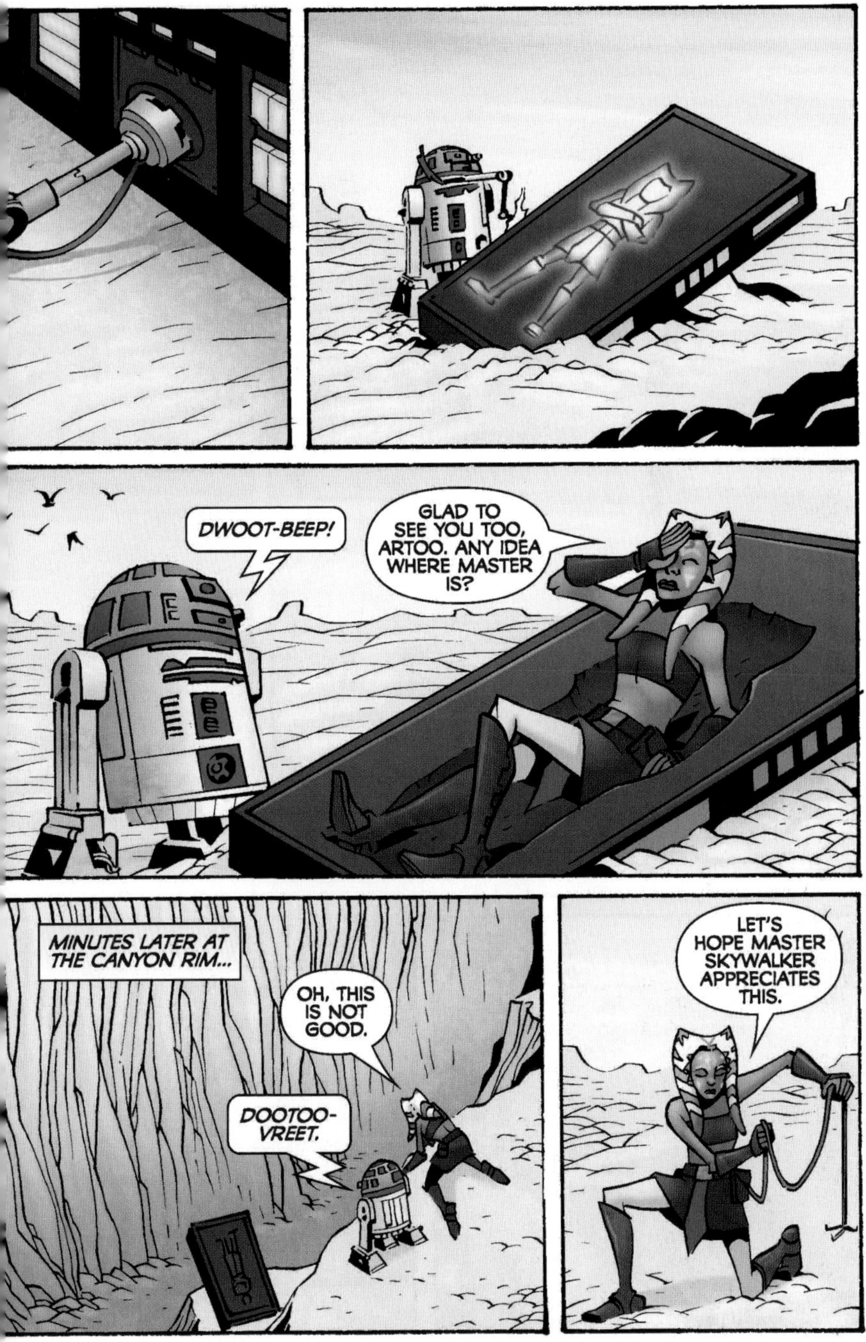
DWOOT-BEEP!
GLAD TO SEE YOU TOO, ARTOO. ANY IDEA WHERE MASTER IS?
MINUTES LATER AT THE CANYON RIM...
OH, THIS IS NOT GOOD.
DOOTOO-VREET.
LET'S HOPE MASTER SKYWALKER APPRECIATES THIS.

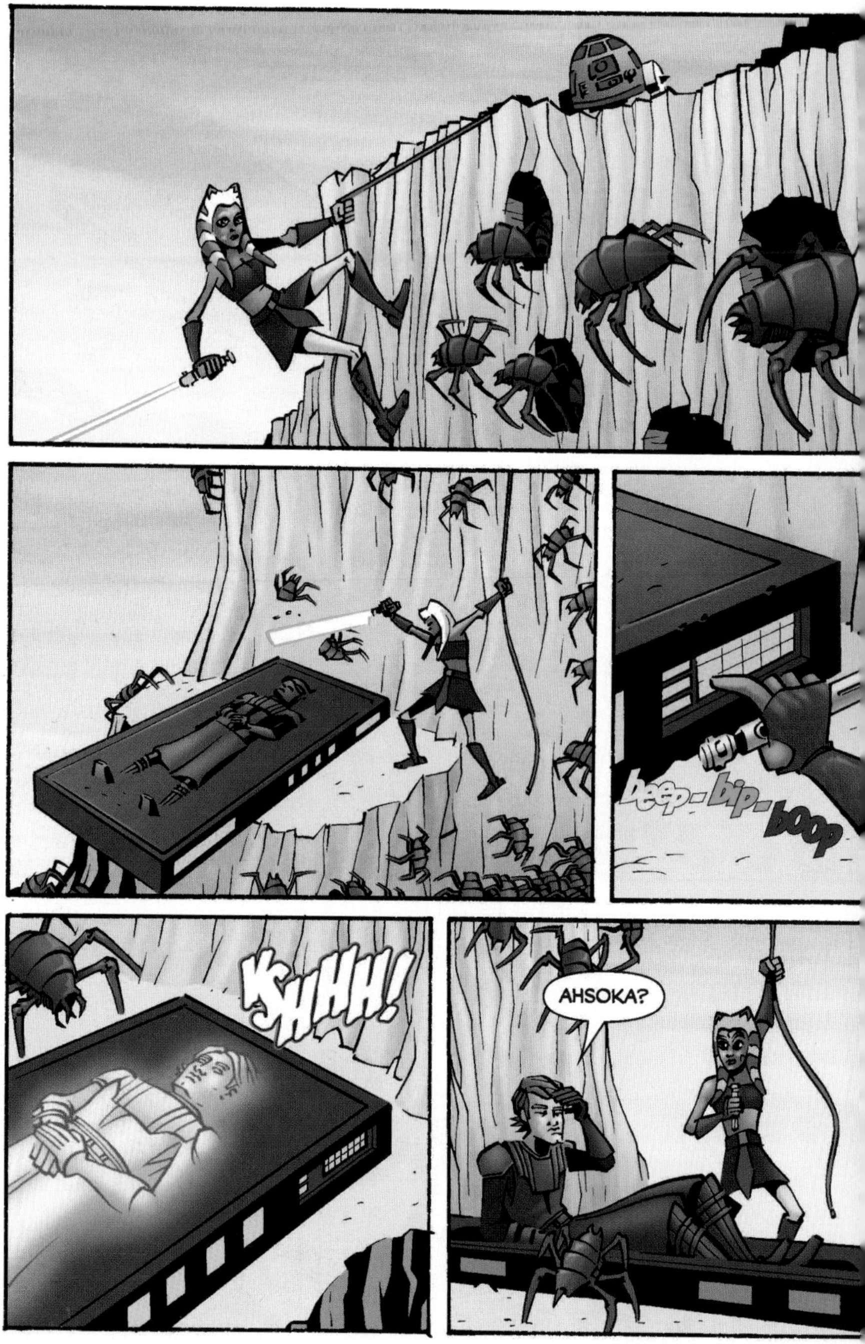
beep-bip-boop
KSHHH!
AHSOKA?

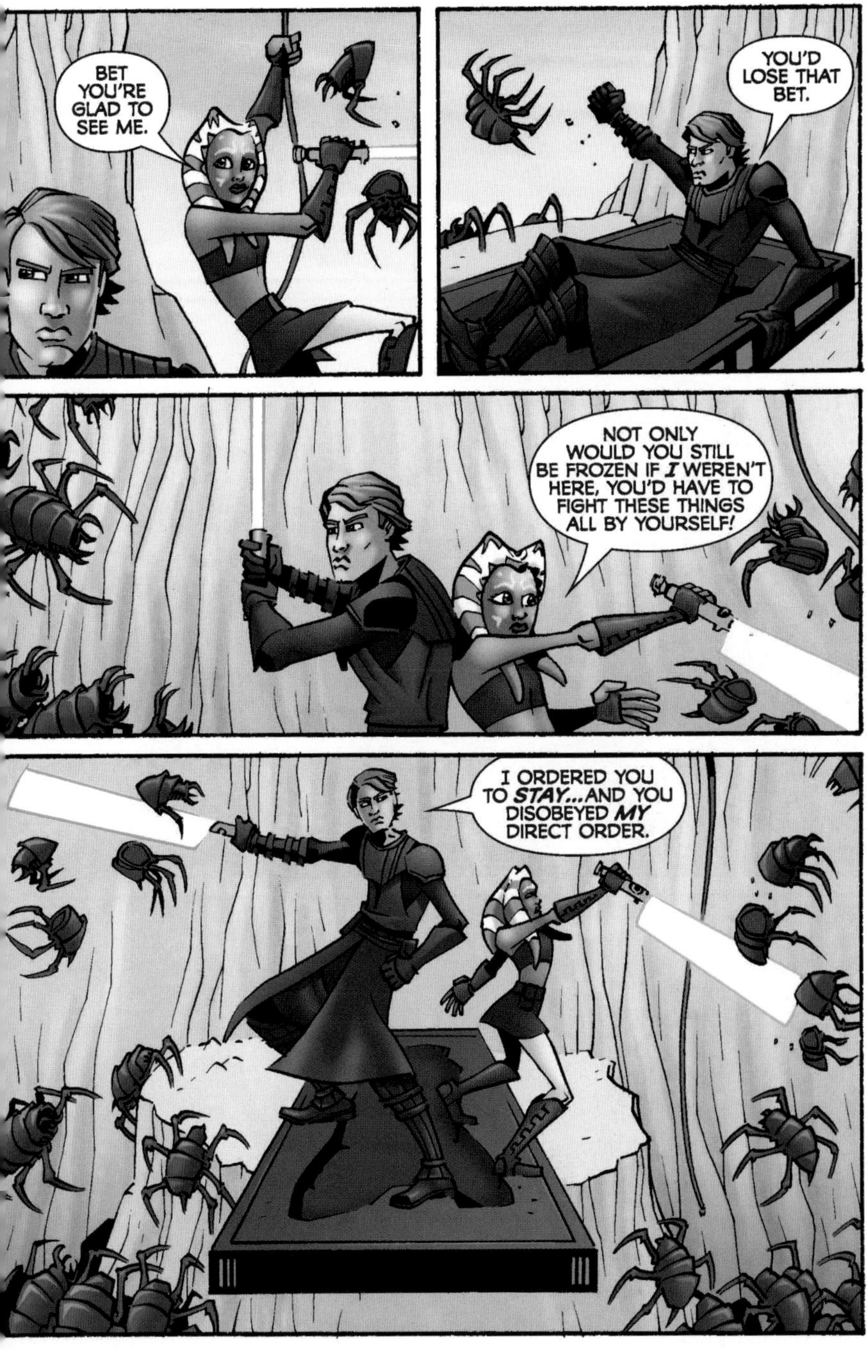
BET YOU'RE GLAD TO SEE ME.
YOU'D LOSE THAT BET.
NOT ONLY WOULD YOU STILL BE FROZEN IF *I* WEREN'T HERE, YOU'D HAVE TO FIGHT THESE THINGS ALL BY YOURSELF!
I ORDERED YOU TO *STAY*...AND YOU DISOBEYED *MY* DIRECT ORDER.

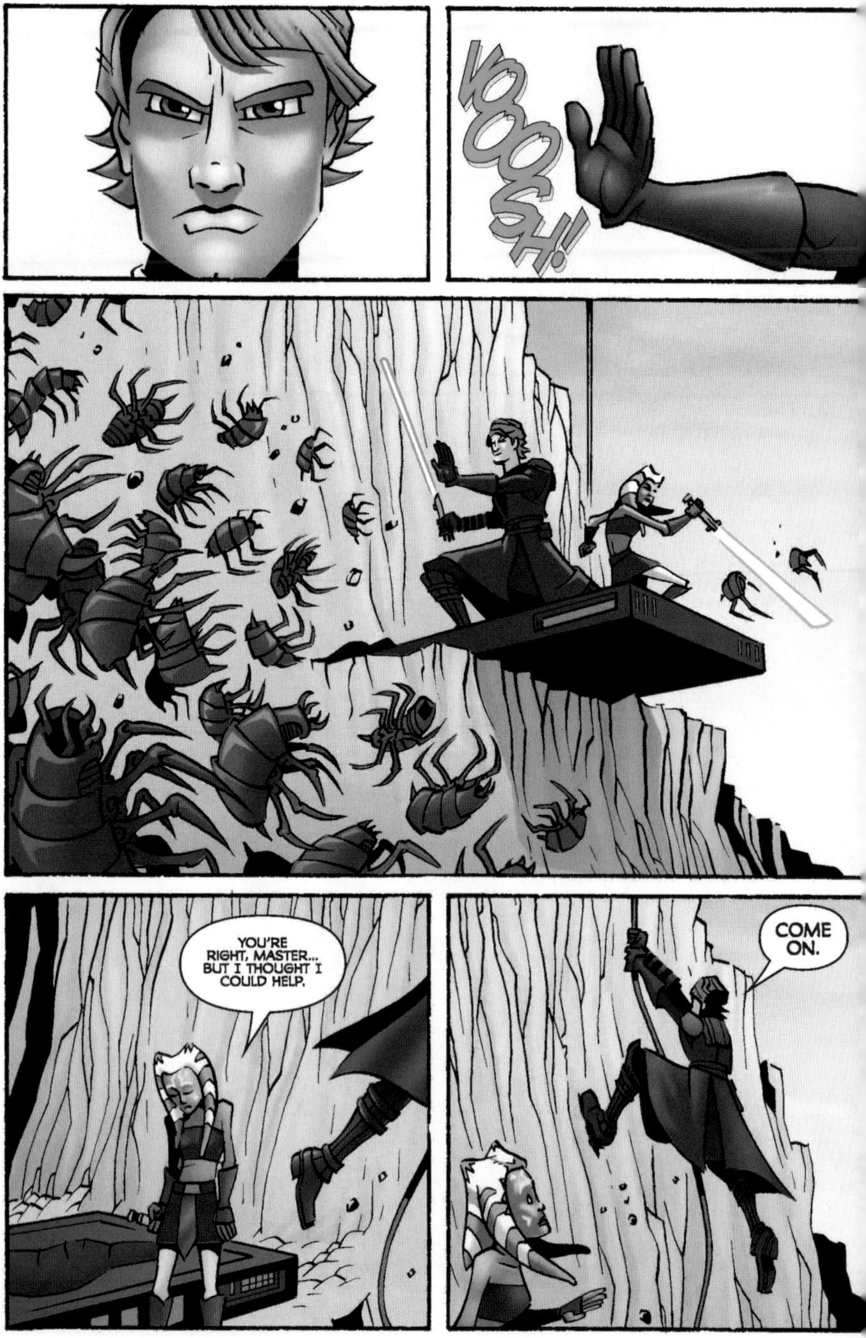
VOOOSH!
YOU'RE RIGHT, MASTER... BUT I THOUGHT I COULD HELP.
COME ON.

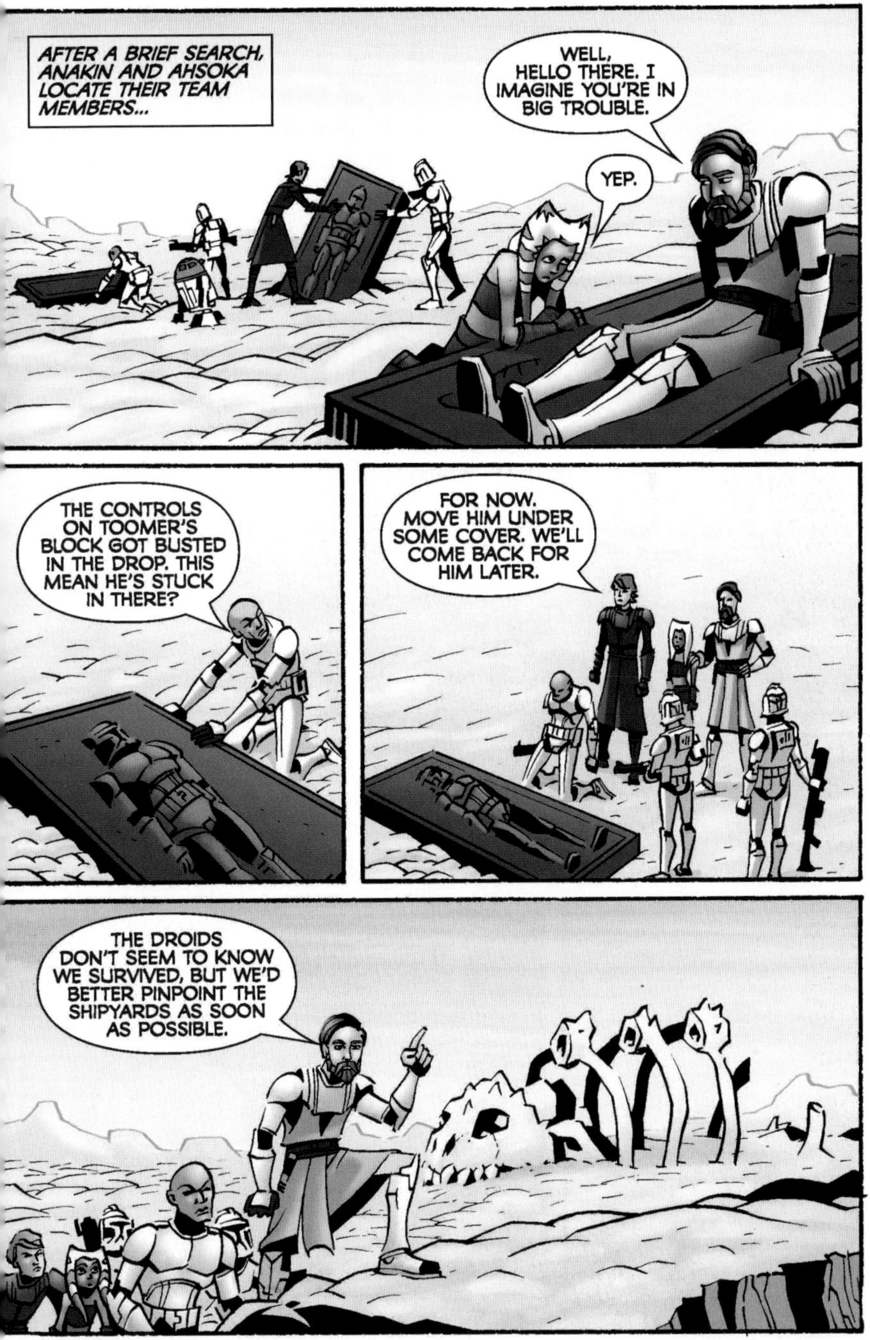
AFTER A BRIEF SEARCH, ANAKIN AND AHSOKA LOCATE THEIR TEAM MEMBERS...
WELL, HELLO THERE. I IMAGINE YOU'RE IN BIG TROUBLE.
YEP.
THE CONTROLS ON TOOMER'S BLOCK GOT BUSTED IN THE DROP. THIS MEAN HE'S STUCK IN THERE?
FOR NOW. MOVE HIM UNDER SOME COVER. WE'LL COME BACK FOR HIM LATER.
THE DROIDS DON'T SEEM TO KNOW WE SURVIVED, BUT WE'D BETTER PINPOINT THE SHIPYARDS AS SOON AS POSSIBLE.

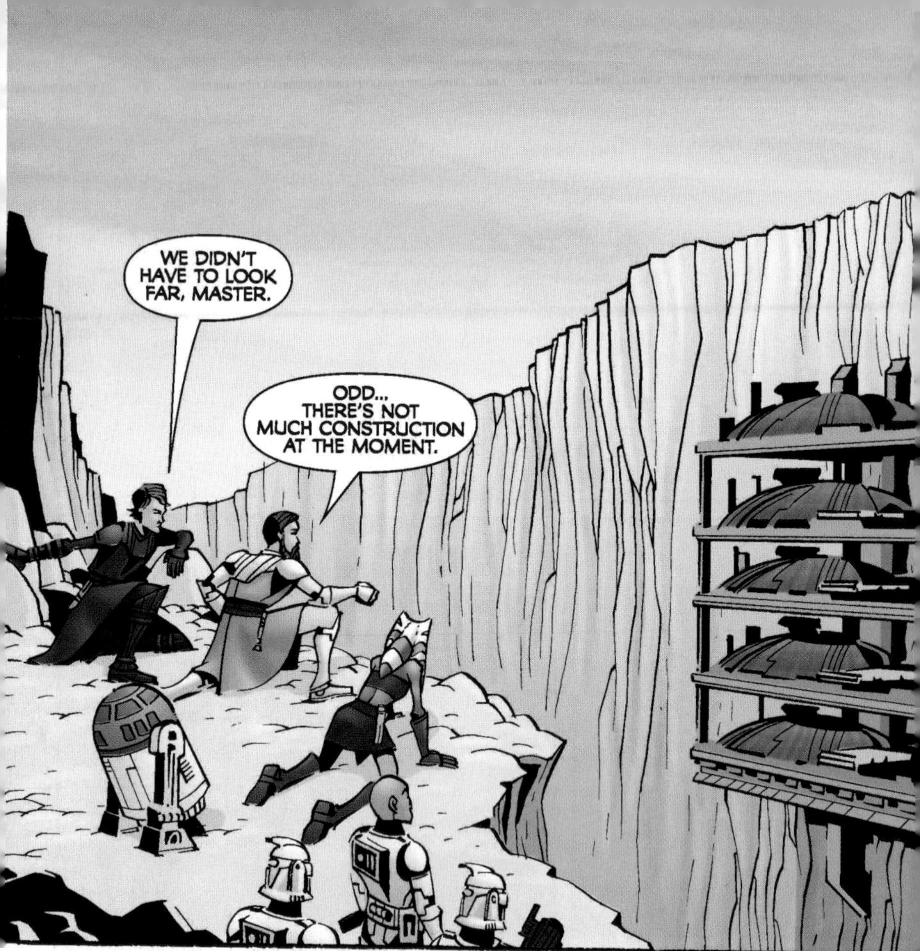
WE DIDN'T HAVE TO LOOK FAR, MASTER.
ODD... THERE'S NOT MUCH CONSTRUCTION AT THE MOMENT.

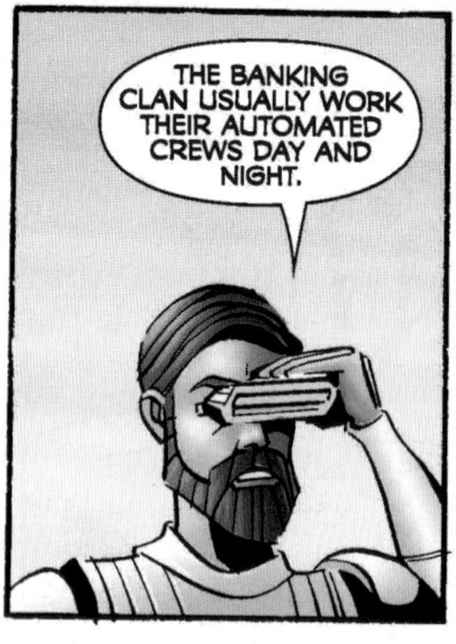
THE BANKING CLAN USUALLY WORK THEIR AUTOMATED CREWS DAY AND NIGHT.

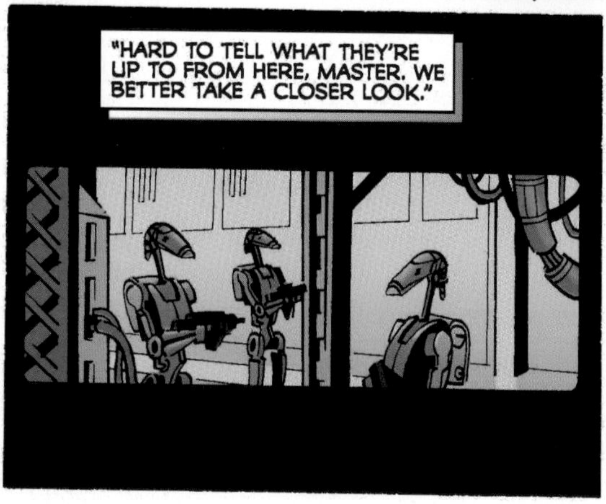
"HARD TO TELL WHAT THEY'RE UP TO FROM HERE, MASTER. WE BETTER TAKE A CLOSER LOOK."

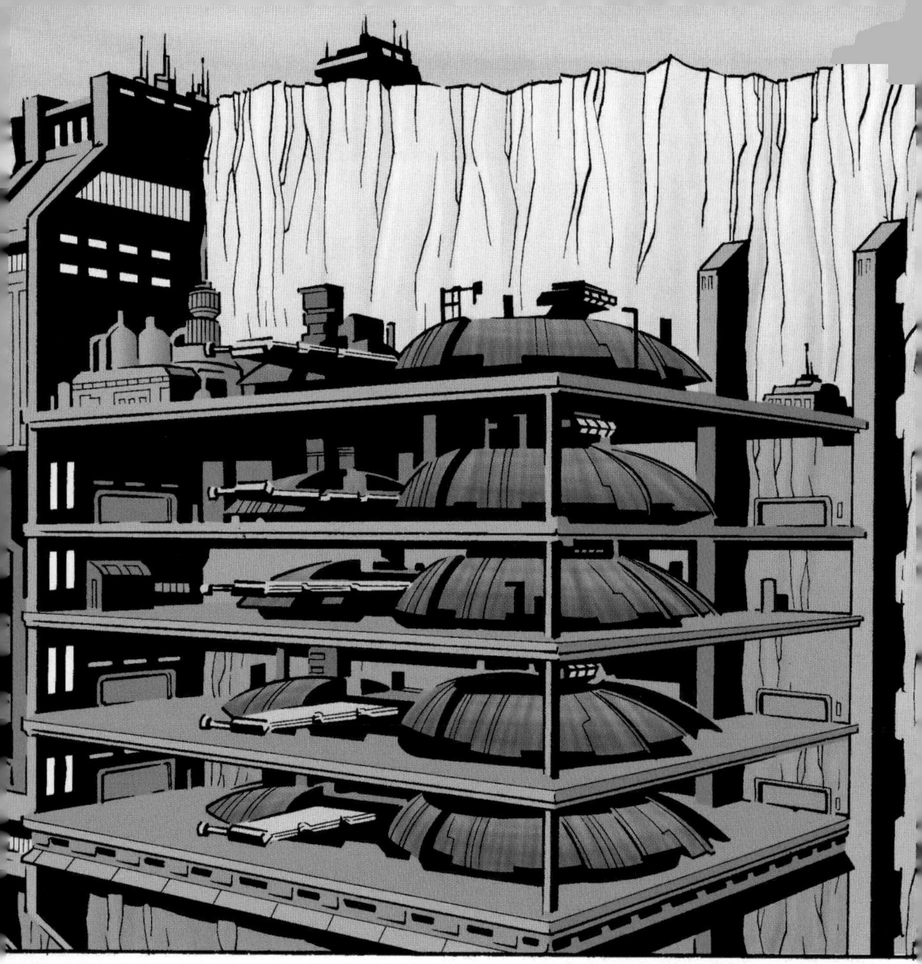

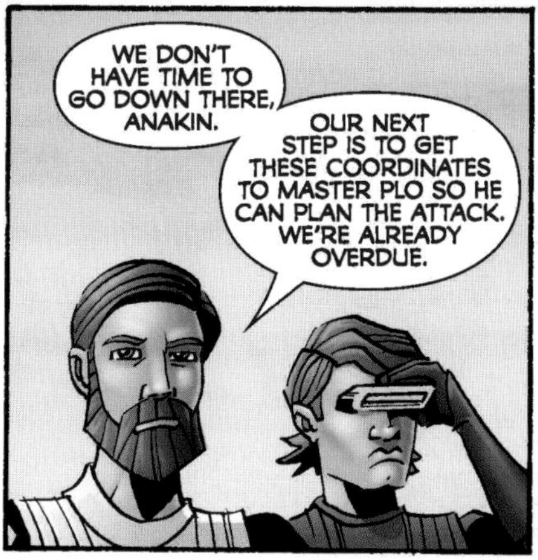

WE DON'T HAVE TIME TO GO DOWN THERE, ANAKIN.
OUR NEXT STEP IS TO GET THESE COORDINATES TO MASTER PLO SO HE CAN PLAN THE ATTACK. WE'RE ALREADY OVERDUE.

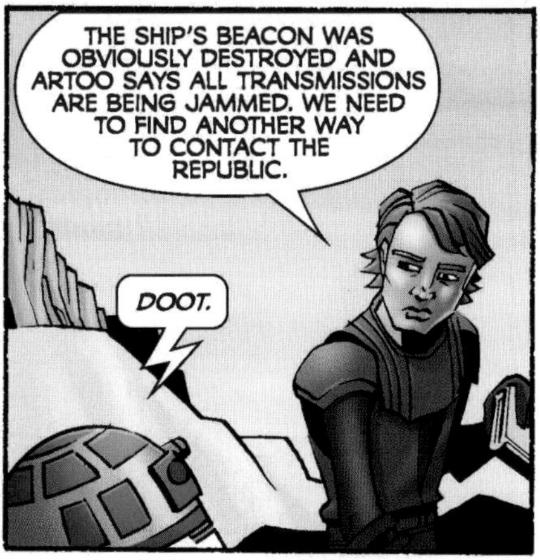

THE SHIP'S BEACON WAS OBVIOUSLY DESTROYED AND ARTOO SAYS ALL TRANSMISSIONS ARE BEING JAMMED. WE NEED TO FIND ANOTHER WAY TO CONTACT THE REPUBLIC.
DOOT.

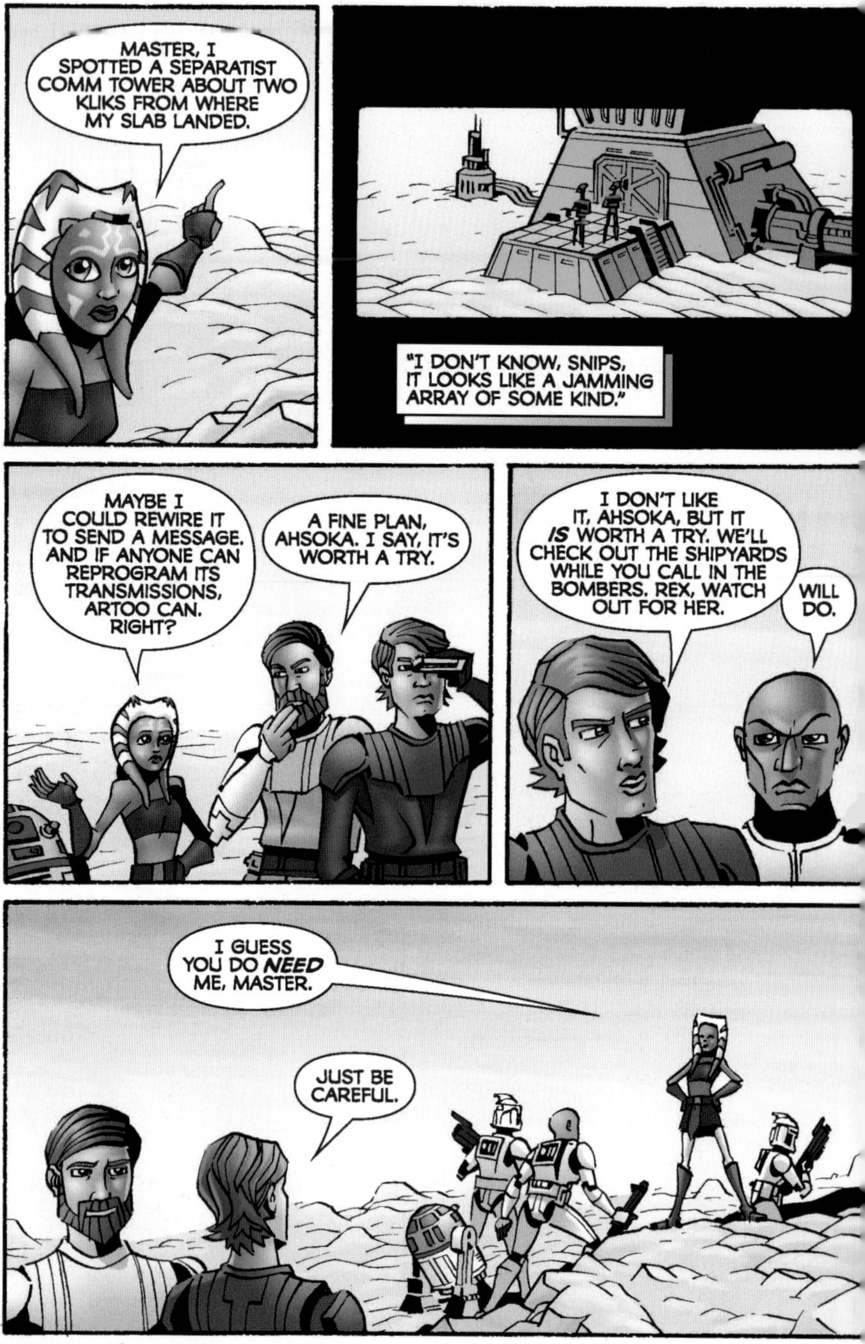
MASTER, I SPOTTED A SEPARATIST COMM TOWER ABOUT TWO KLIKS FROM WHERE MY SLAB LANDED.
"I DON'T KNOW, SNIPS, IT LOOKS LIKE A JAMMING ARRAY OF SOME KIND."
MAYBE I COULD REWIRE IT TO SEND A MESSAGE. AND IF ANYONE CAN REPROGRAM ITS TRANSMISSIONS, ARTOO CAN. RIGHT?
A FINE PLAN, AHSOKA. I SAY, IT'S WORTH A TRY.
I DON'T LIKE IT, AHSOKA, BUT IT *IS* WORTH A TRY. WE'LL CHECK OUT THE SHIPYARDS WHILE YOU CALL IN THE BOMBERS. REX, WATCH OUT FOR HER.
WILL DO.
I GUESS YOU DO ***NEED*** ME, MASTER.
JUST BE CAREFUL.

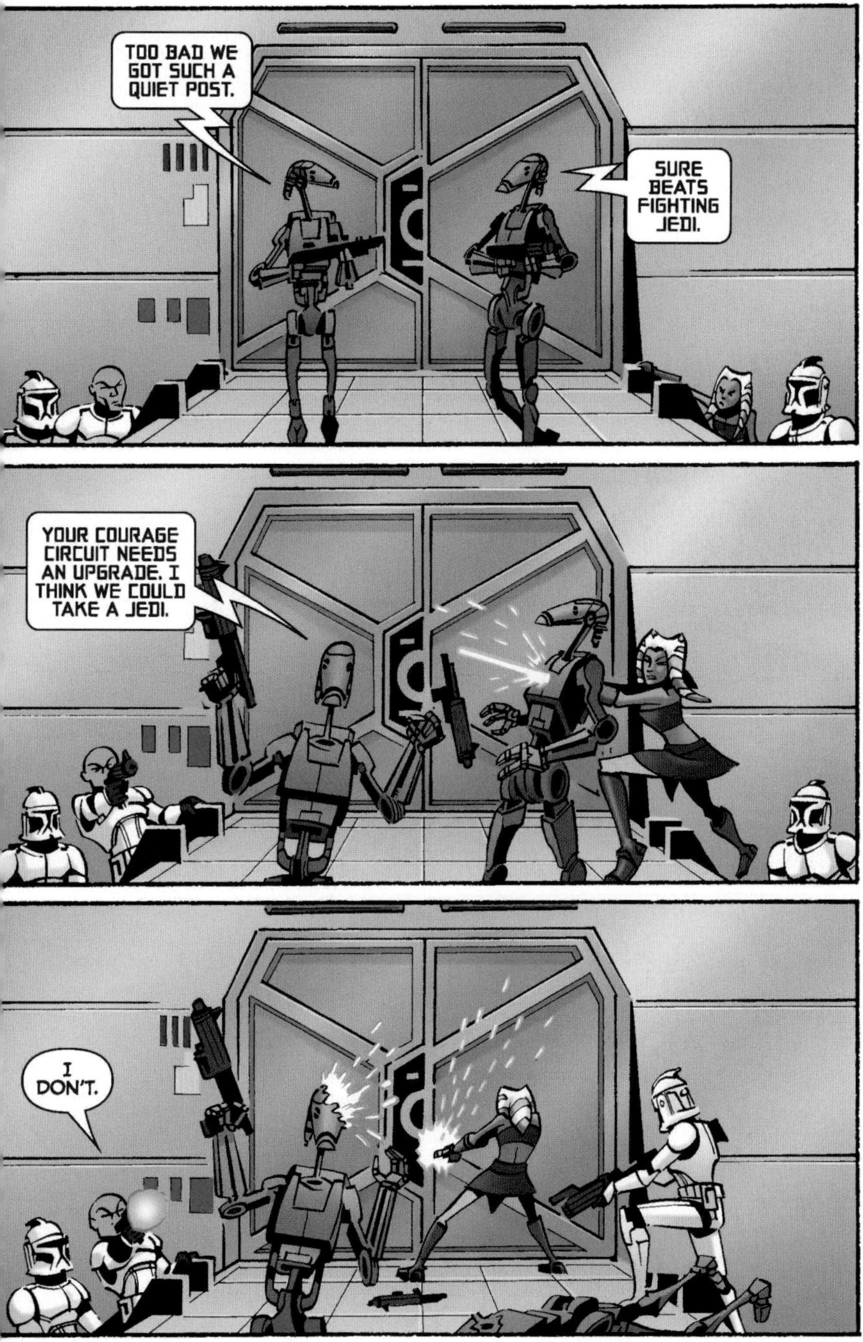
TOO BAD WE GOT SUCH A QUIET POST.
SURE BEATS FIGHTING JEDI.
YOUR COURAGE CIRCUIT NEEDS AN UPGRADE. I THINK WE COULD TAKE A JEDI.
I DON'T.

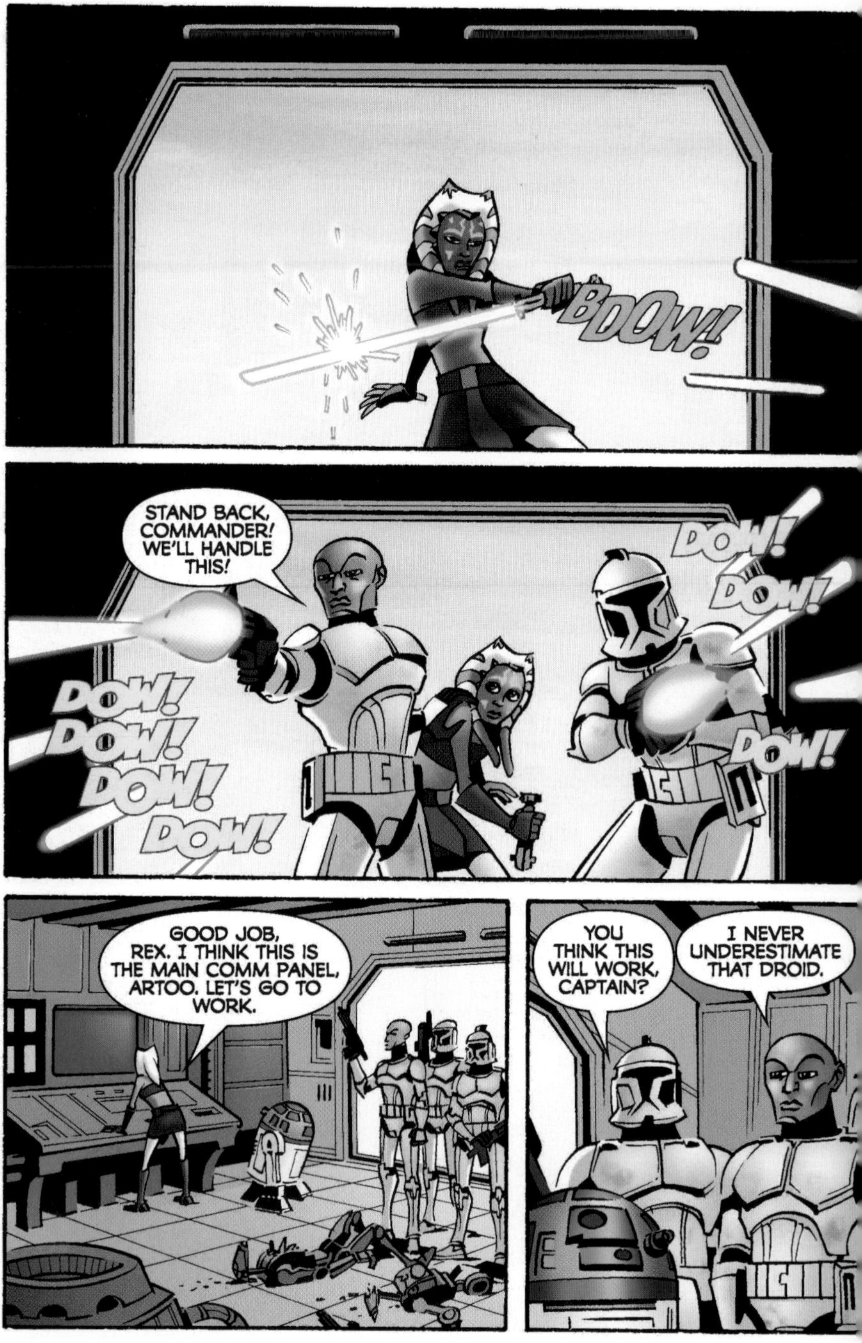
BDOW!!
STAND BACK, COMMANDER! WE'LL HANDLE THIS!
DOW! DOW!
DOW! DOW! DOW! DOW!
DOW!
GOOD JOB, REX. I THINK THIS IS THE MAIN COMM PANEL, ARTOO. LET'S GO TO WORK.
YOU THINK THIS WILL WORK, CAPTAIN?
I NEVER UNDERESTIMATE THAT DROID.

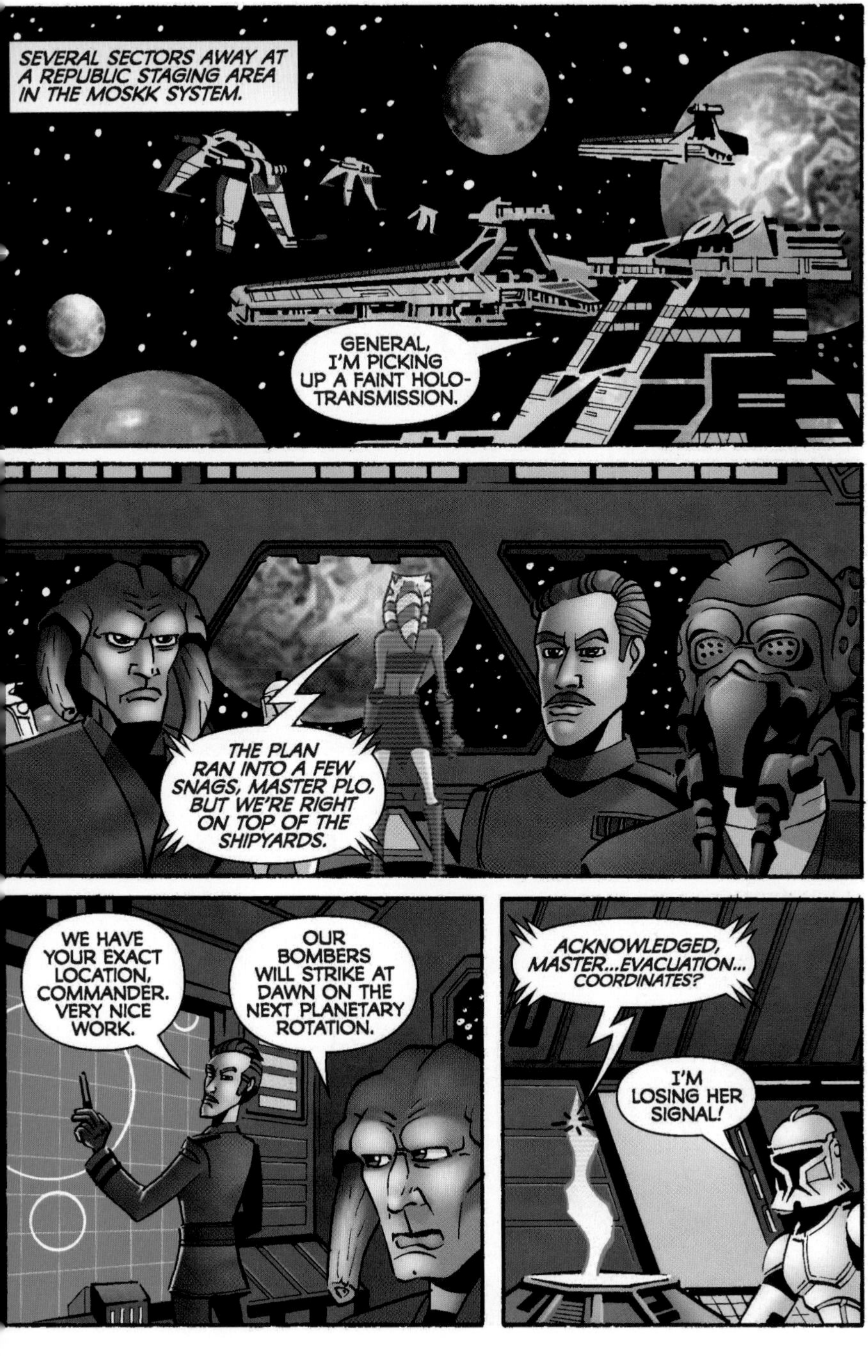
SEVERAL SECTORS AWAY AT A REPUBLIC STAGING AREA IN THE MOSKK SYSTEM.
GENERAL, I'M PICKING UP A FAINT HOLO-TRANSMISSION.
THE PLAN RAN INTO A FEW SNAGS, MASTER PLO, BUT WE'RE RIGHT ON TOP OF THE SHIPYARDS.
WE HAVE YOUR EXACT LOCATION, COMMANDER. VERY NICE WORK.
OUR BOMBERS WILL STRIKE AT DAWN ON THE NEXT PLANETARY ROTATION.
ACKNOWLEDGED, MASTER...EVACUATION... COORDINATES?
I'M LOSING HER SIGNAL!

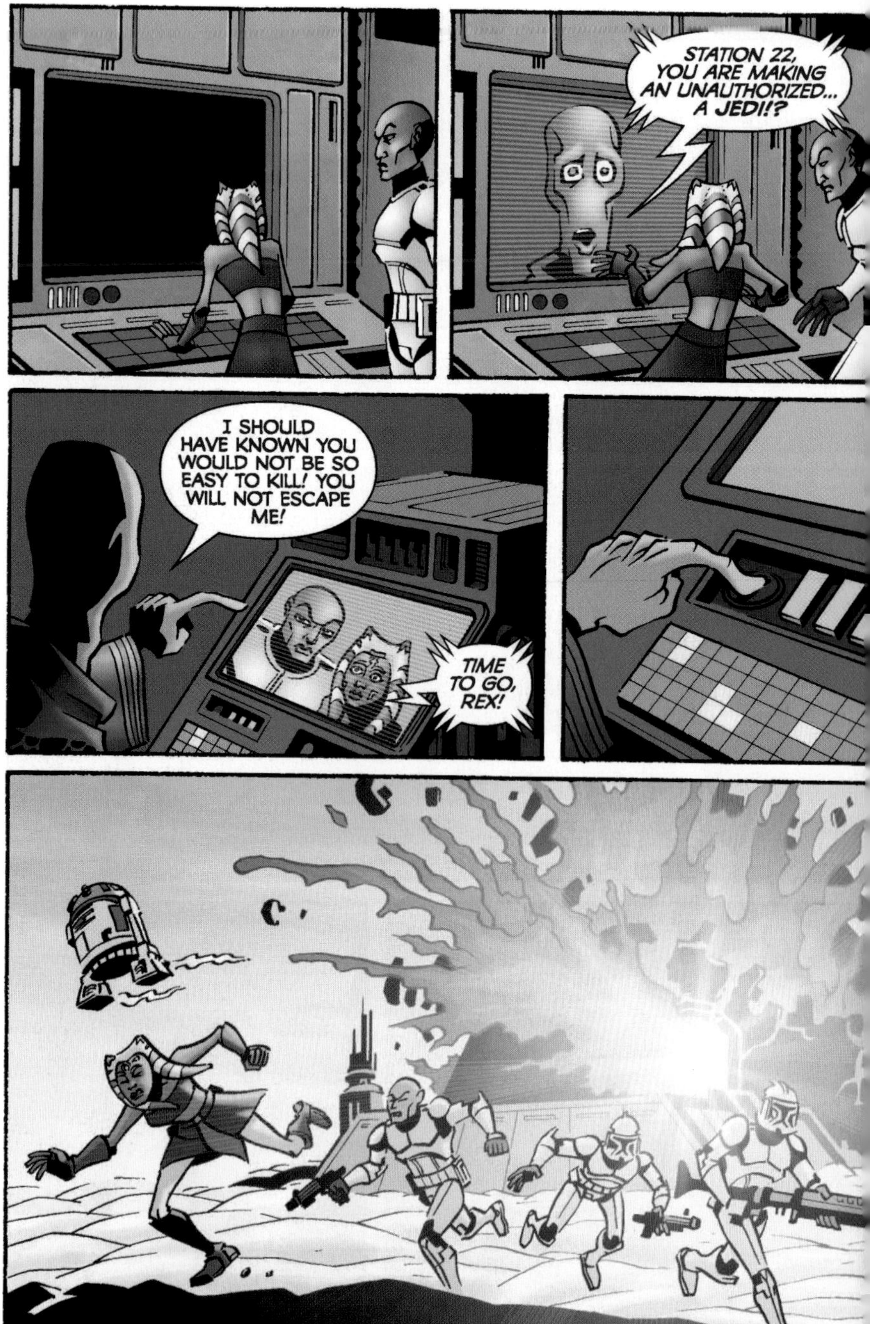
STATION 22, YOU ARE MAKING AN UNAUTHORIZED... A JEDI!?
I SHOULD HAVE KNOWN YOU WOULD NOT BE SO EASY TO KILL! YOU WILL NOT ESCAPE ME!
TIME TO GO, REX!

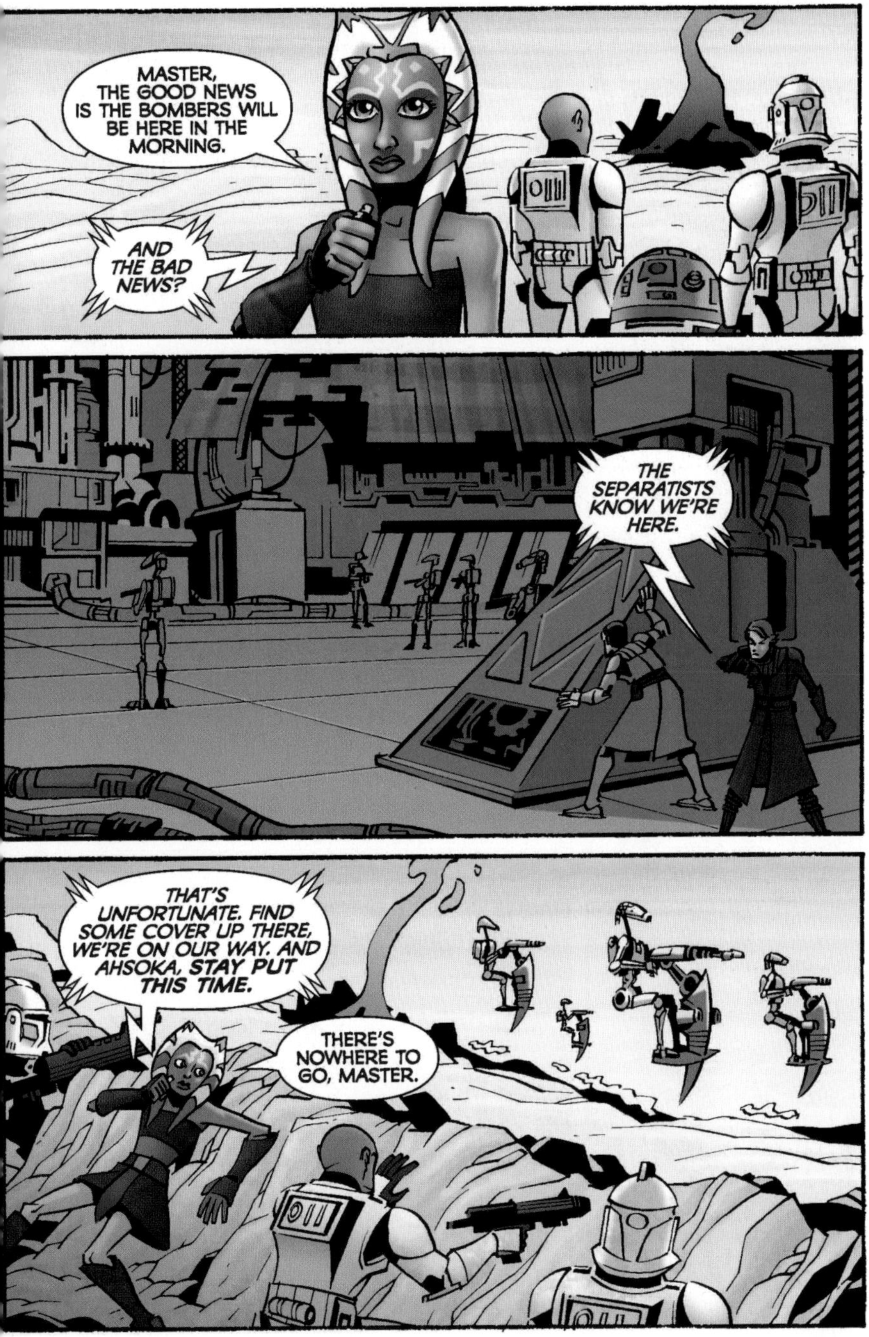
MASTER, THE GOOD NEWS IS THE BOMBERS WILL BE HERE IN THE MORNING.
AND THE BAD NEWS?
THE SEPARATISTS KNOW WE'RE HERE.
THAT'S UNFORTUNATE. FIND SOME COVER UP THERE, WE'RE ON OUR WAY. AND AHSOKA, STAY PUT THIS TIME.
THERE'S NOWHERE TO GO, MASTER.

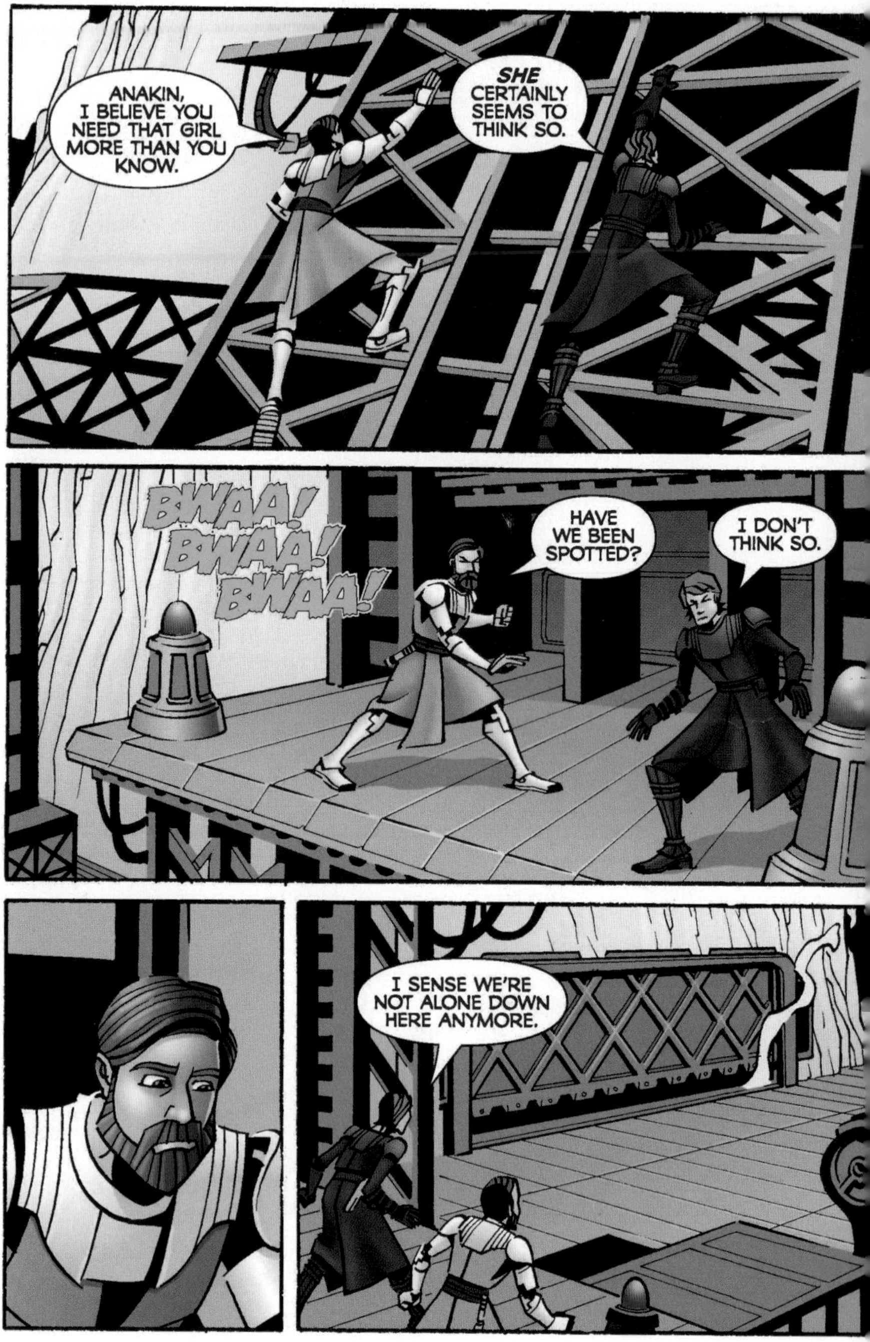
ANAKIN, I BELIEVE YOU NEED THAT GIRL MORE THAN YOU KNOW.
SHE CERTAINLY SEEMS TO THINK SO.
BWAA! BWAA! BWAA!
HAVE WE BEEN SPOTTED?
I DON'T THINK SO.
I SENSE WE'RE NOT ALONE DOWN HERE ANYMORE.

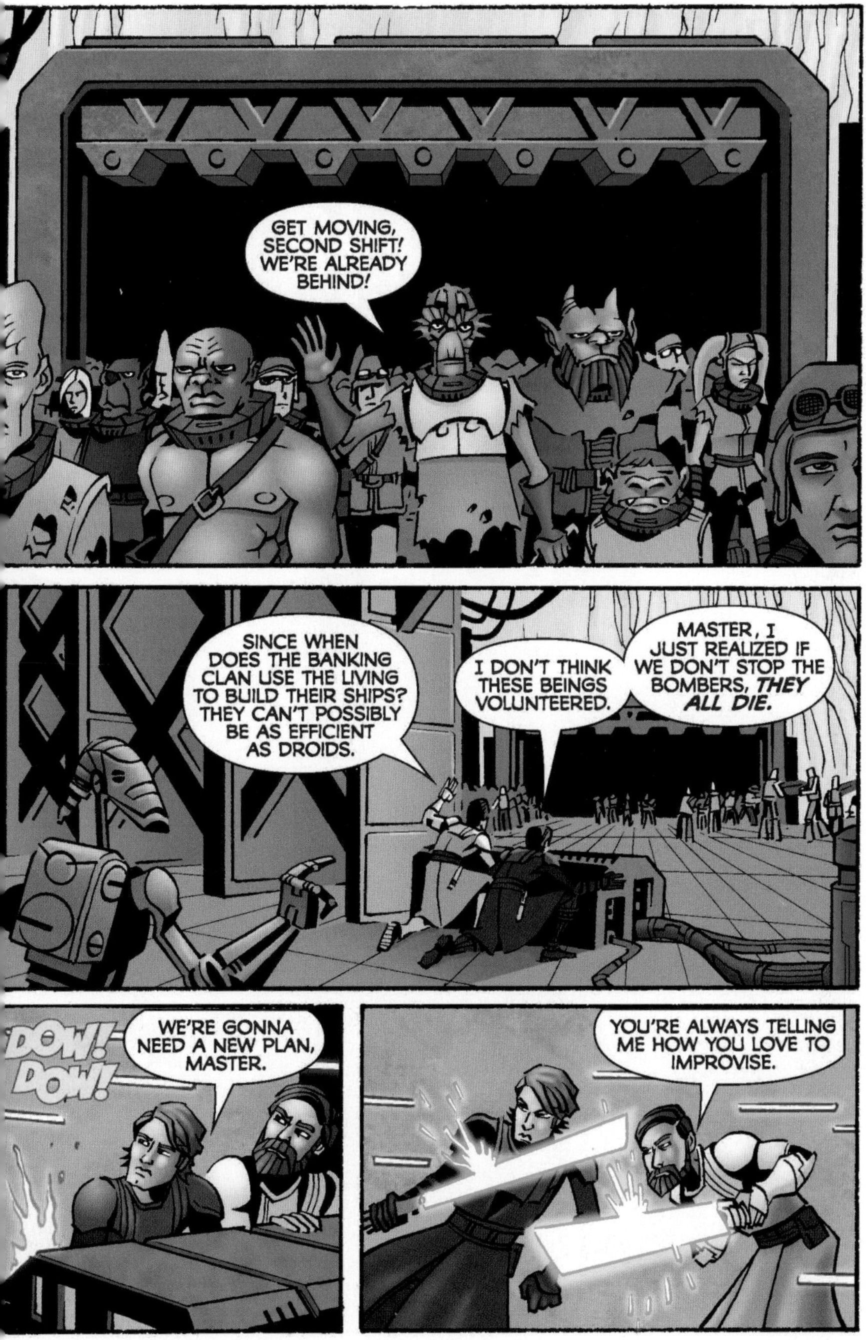
GET MOVING, SECOND SHIFT! WE'RE ALREADY BEHIND!
SINCE WHEN DOES THE BANKING CLAN USE THE LIVING TO BUILD THEIR SHIPS? THEY CAN'T POSSIBLY BE AS EFFICIENT AS DROIDS.
I DON'T THINK THESE BEINGS VOLUNTEERED.
MASTER, I JUST REALIZED IF WE DON'T STOP THE BOMBERS, *THEY ALL DIE.*
DOW! DOW!
WE'RE GONNA NEED A NEW PLAN, MASTER.
YOU'RE ALWAYS TELLING ME HOW YOU LOVE TO IMPROVISE.

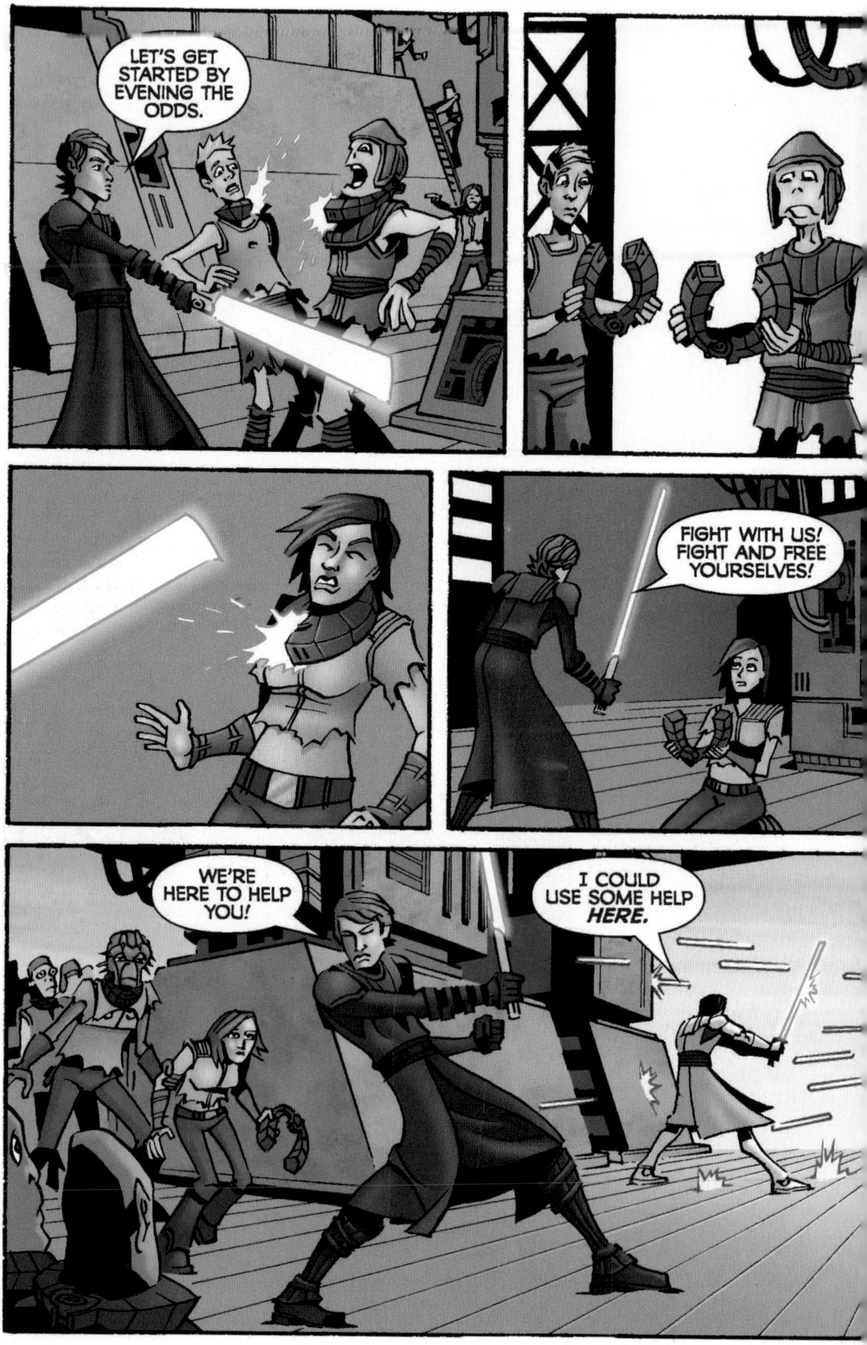
LET'S GET STARTED BY EVENING THE ODDS.
FIGHT WITH US! FIGHT AND FREE YOURSELVES!
WE'RE HERE TO HELP YOU!
I COULD USE SOME HELP *HERE.*

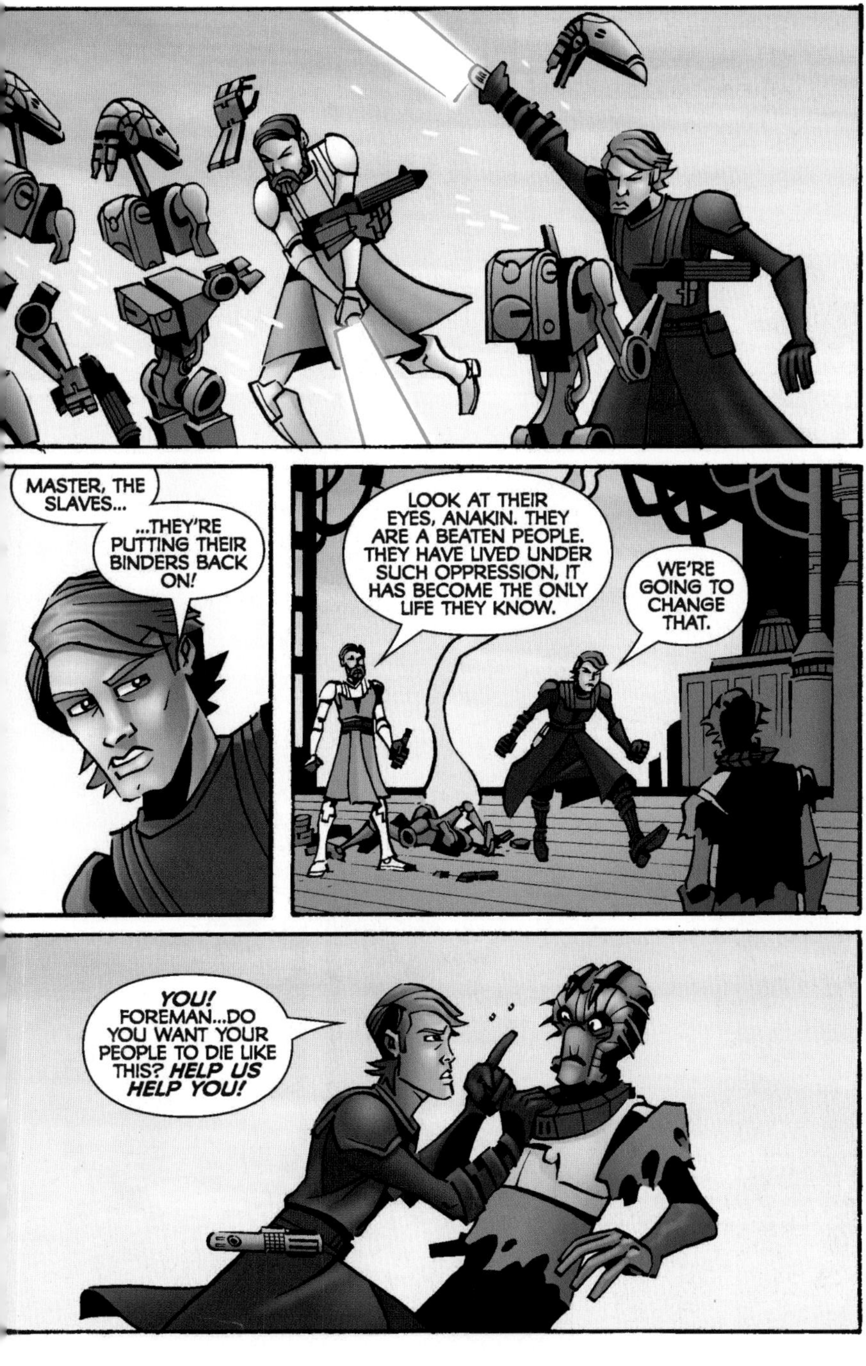
MASTER, THE SLAVES...
...THEY'RE PUTTING THEIR BINDERS BACK ON!
LOOK AT THEIR EYES, ANAKIN. THEY ARE A BEATEN PEOPLE. THEY HAVE LIVED UNDER SUCH OPPRESSION, IT HAS BECOME THE ONLY LIFE THEY KNOW.
WE'RE GOING TO CHANGE THAT.
YOU! FOREMAN...DO YOU WANT YOUR PEOPLE TO DIE LIKE THIS? ***HELP US HELP YOU!***

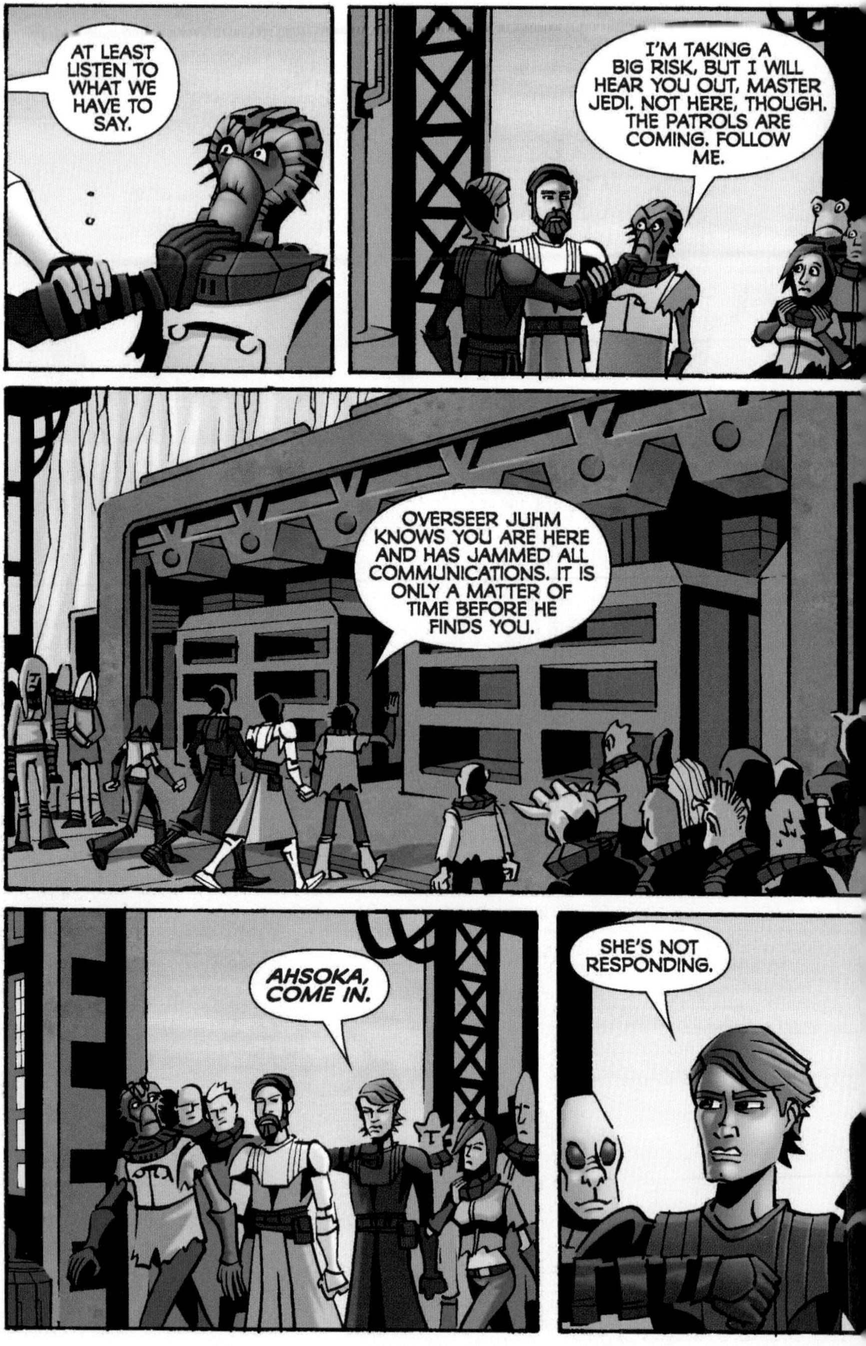
AT LEAST LISTEN TO WHAT WE HAVE TO SAY.
I'M TAKING A BIG RISK, BUT I WILL HEAR YOU OUT, MASTER JEDI. NOT HERE, THOUGH. THE PATROLS ARE COMING. FOLLOW ME.
OVERSEER JUHM KNOWS YOU ARE HERE AND HAS JAMMED ALL COMMUNICATIONS. IT IS ONLY A MATTER OF TIME BEFORE HE FINDS YOU.
AHSOKA, COME IN.
SHE'S NOT RESPONDING.

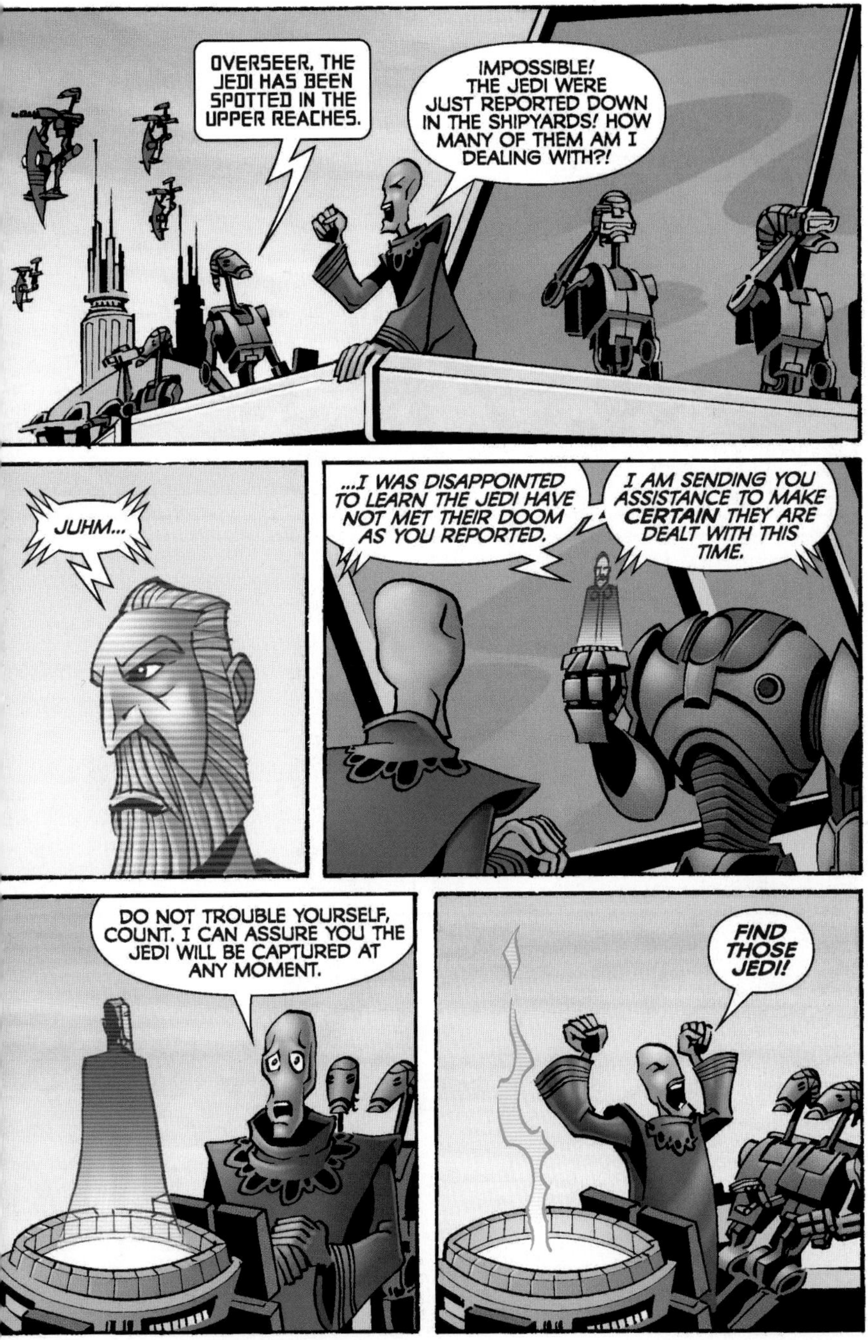
OVERSEER, THE JEDI HAS BEEN SPOTTED IN THE UPPER REACHES.
IMPOSSIBLE! THE JEDI WERE JUST REPORTED DOWN IN THE SHIPYARDS! HOW MANY OF THEM AM I DEALING WITH?!
JUHM...
...I WAS DISAPPOINTED TO LEARN THE JEDI HAVE NOT MET THEIR DOOM AS YOU REPORTED.
I AM SENDING YOU ASSISTANCE TO MAKE CERTAIN THEY ARE DEALT WITH THIS TIME.
DO NOT TROUBLE YOURSELF, COUNT. I CAN ASSURE YOU THE JEDI WILL BE CAPTURED AT ANY MOMENT.
FIND THOSE JEDI!

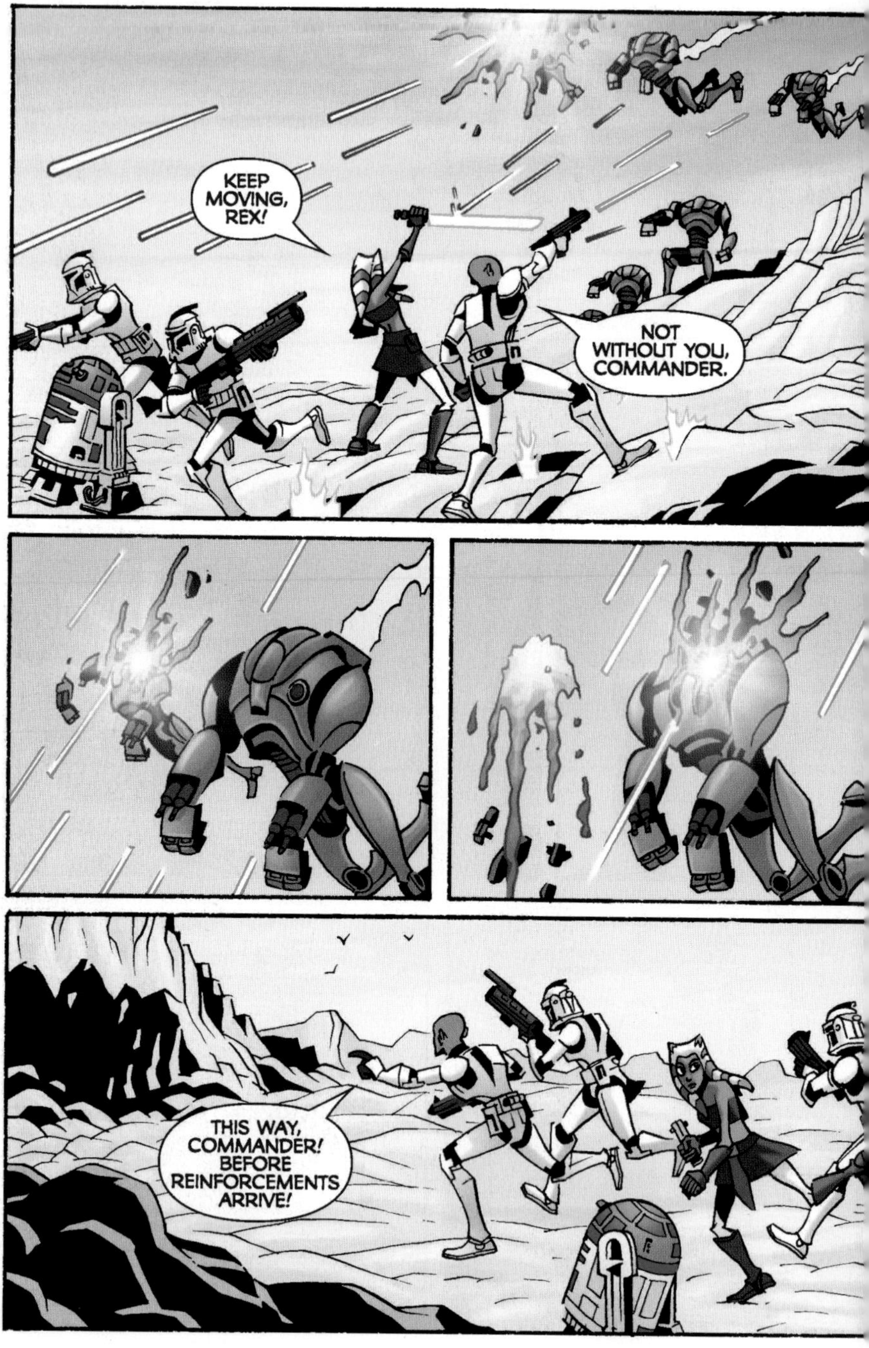
KEEP MOVING, REX!
NOT WITHOUT YOU, COMMANDER.
THIS WAY, COMMANDER! BEFORE REINFORCEMENTS ARRIVE!

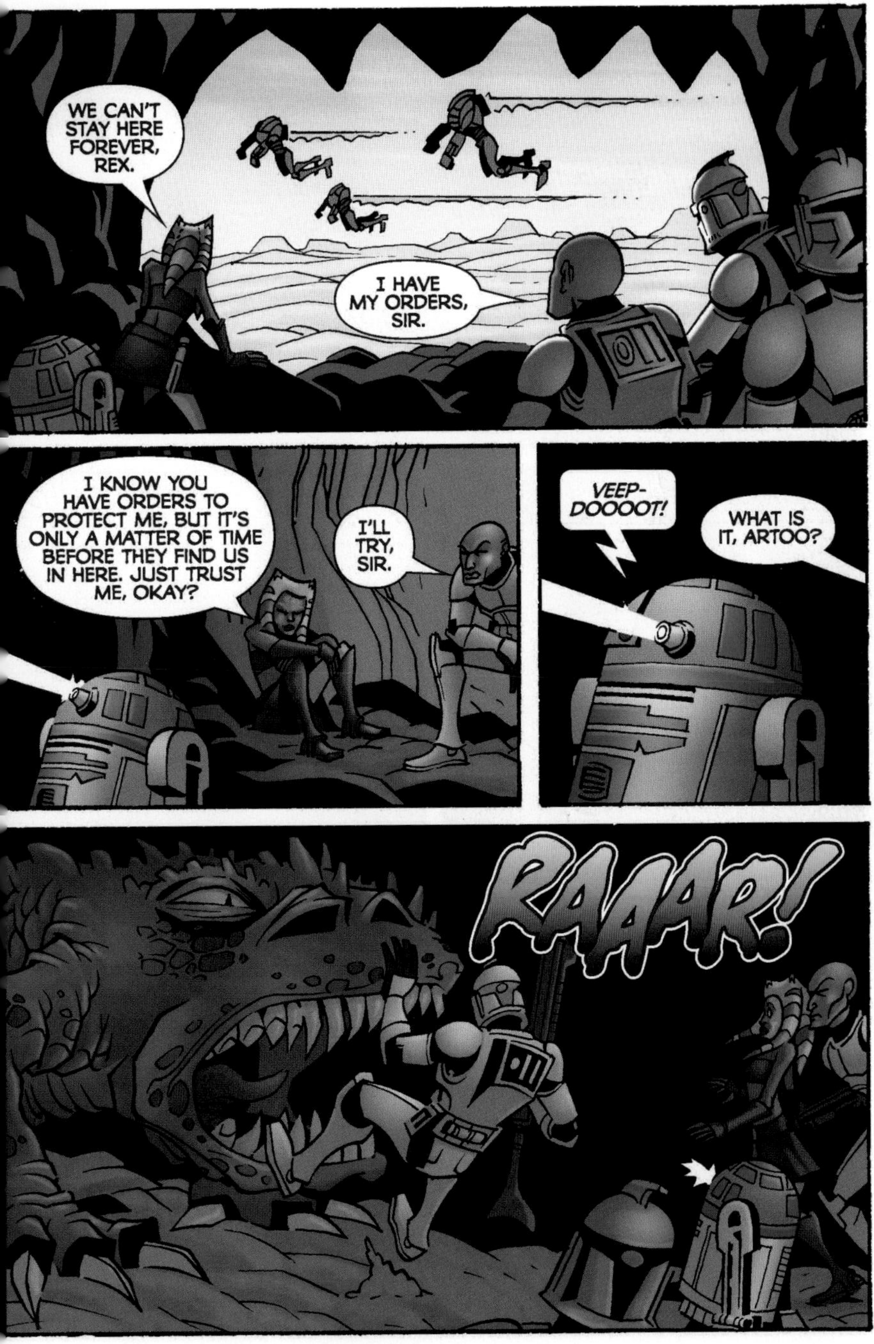
WE CAN'T STAY HERE FOREVER, REX.
I HAVE MY ORDERS, SIR.
I KNOW YOU HAVE ORDERS TO PROTECT ME, BUT IT'S ONLY A MATTER OF TIME BEFORE THEY FIND US IN HERE. JUST TRUST ME, OKAY?
I'LL TRY, SIR.
VEEP-DOOOOT!
WHAT IS IT, ARTOO?
RAAAR!

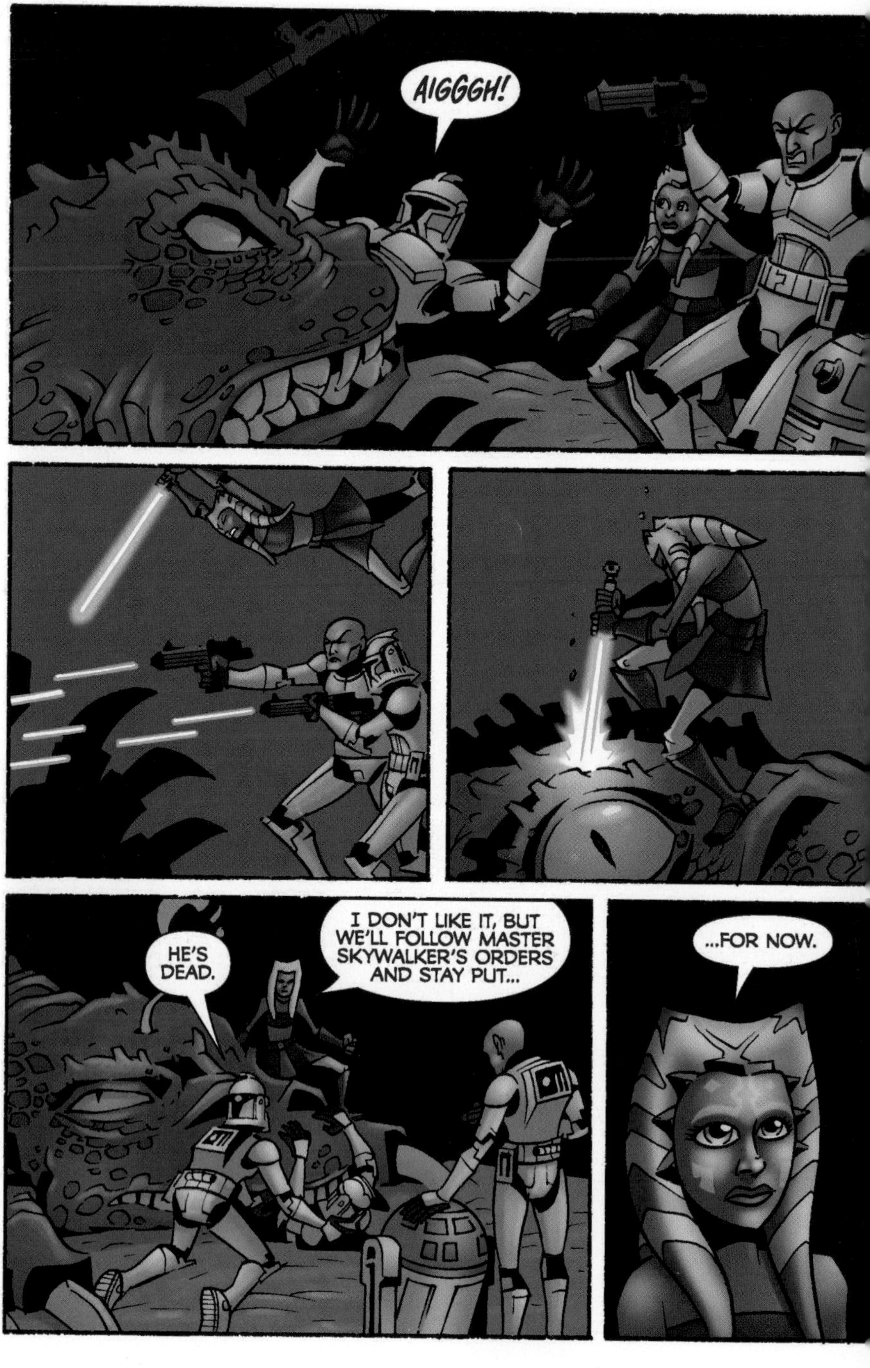
AIGGGH!
HE'S DEAD.
I DON'T LIKE IT, BUT WE'LL FOLLOW MASTER SKYWALKER'S ORDERS AND STAY PUT...
...FOR NOW.

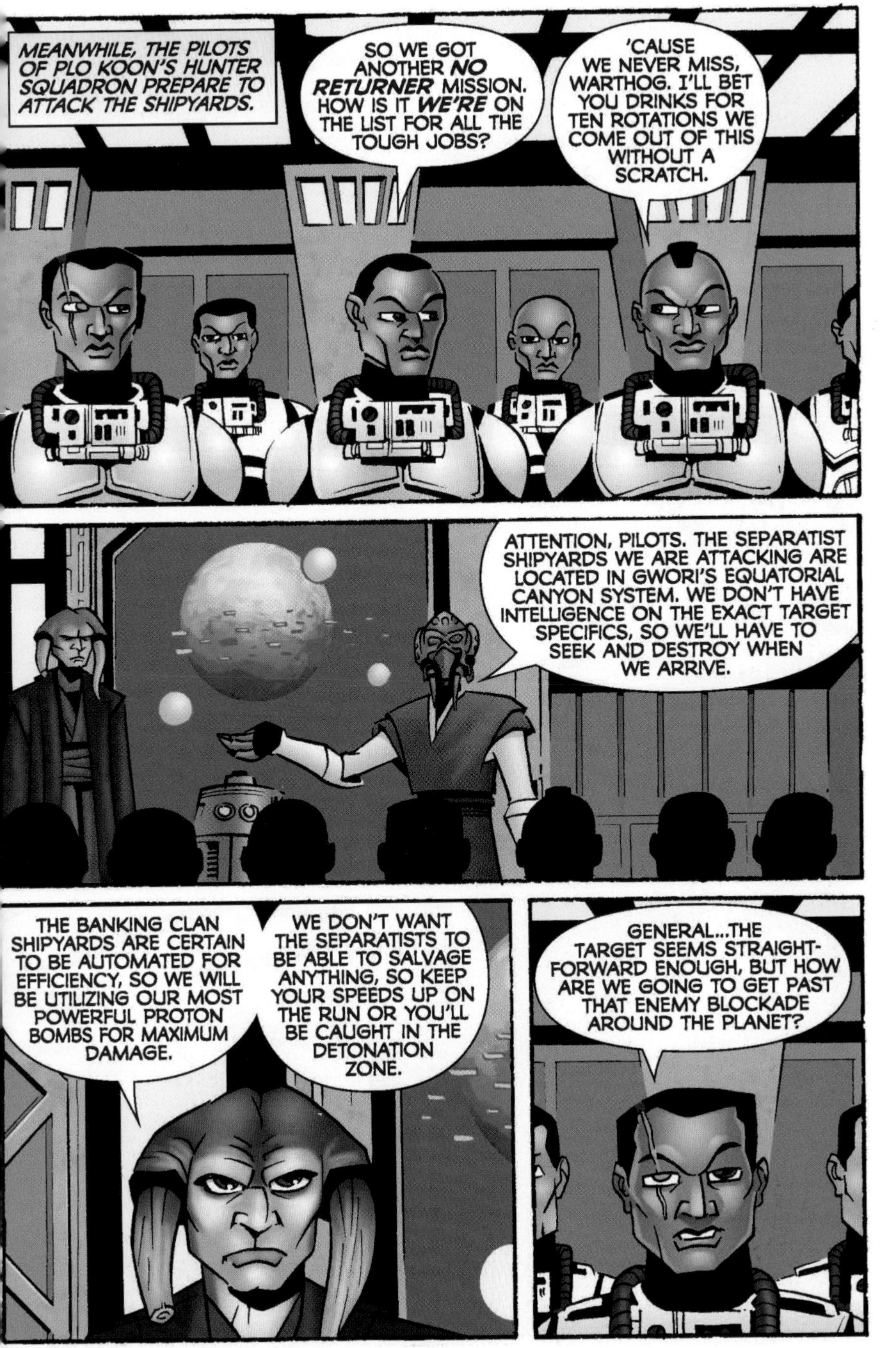
MEANWHILE, THE PILOTS OF PLO KOON'S HUNTER SQUADRON PREPARE TO ATTACK THE SHIPYARDS.
SO WE GOT ANOTHER NO RETURNER MISSION. HOW IS IT WE'RE ON THE LIST FOR ALL THE TOUGH JOBS?
'CAUSE WE NEVER MISS, WARTHOG. I'LL BET YOU DRINKS FOR TEN ROTATIONS WE COME OUT OF THIS WITHOUT A SCRATCH.
ATTENTION, PILOTS. THE SEPARATIST SHIPYARDS WE ARE ATTACKING ARE LOCATED IN GWORI'S EQUATORIAL CANYON SYSTEM. WE DON'T HAVE INTELLIGENCE ON THE EXACT TARGET SPECIFICS, SO WE'LL HAVE TO SEEK AND DESTROY WHEN WE ARRIVE.
THE BANKING CLAN SHIPYARDS ARE CERTAIN TO BE AUTOMATED FOR EFFICIENCY, SO WE WILL BE UTILIZING OUR MOST POWERFUL PROTON BOMBS FOR MAXIMUM DAMAGE.
WE DON'T WANT THE SEPARATISTS TO BE ABLE TO SALVAGE ANYTHING, SO KEEP YOUR SPEEDS UP ON THE RUN OR YOU'LL BE CAUGHT IN THE DETONATION ZONE.
GENERAL...THE TARGET SEEMS STRAIGHT-FORWARD ENOUGH, BUT HOW ARE WE GOING TO GET PAST THAT ENEMY BLOCKADE AROUND THE PLANET?

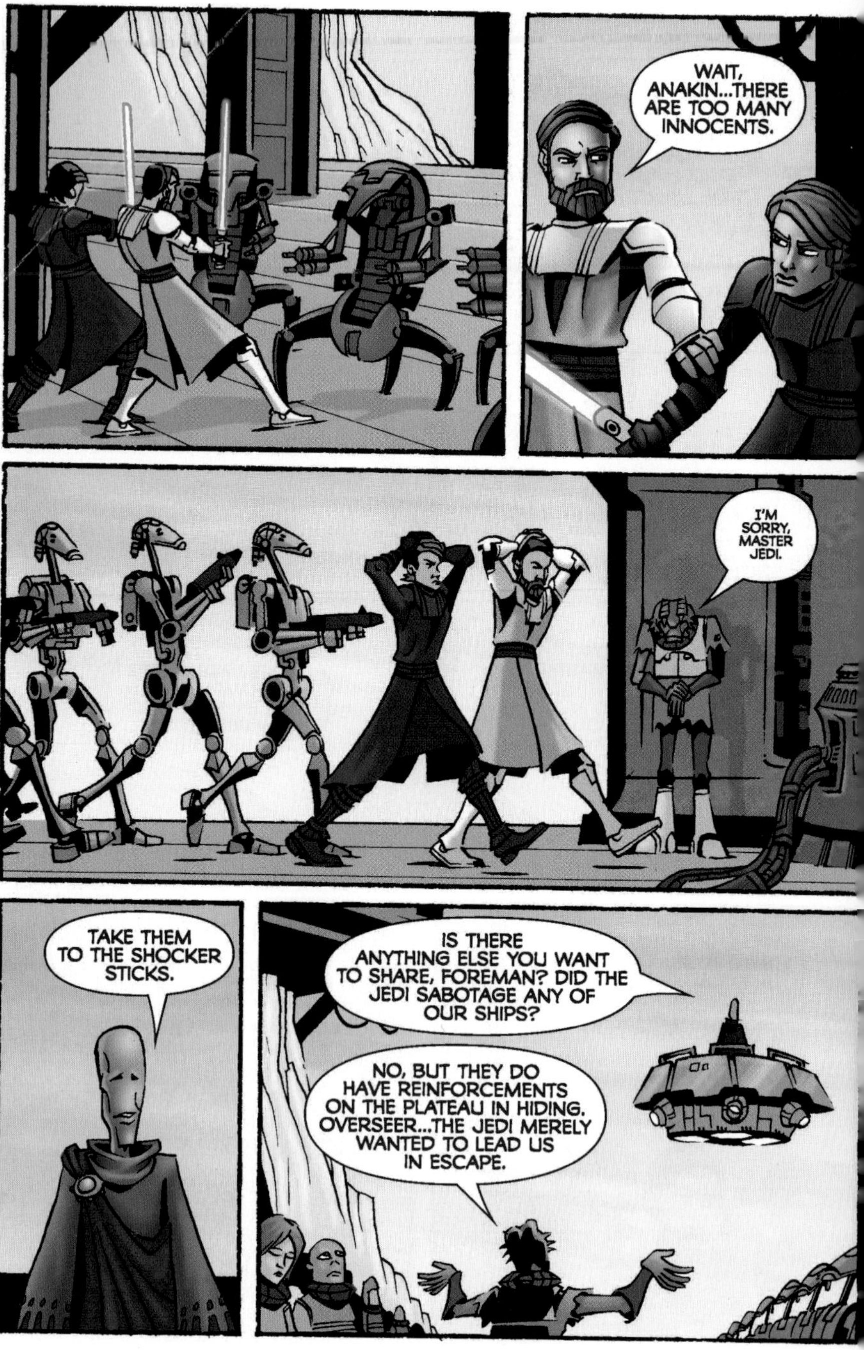
WAIT, ANAKIN...THERE ARE TOO MANY INNOCENTS.
I'M SORRY, MASTER JEDI.
TAKE THEM TO THE SHOCKER STICKS.
IS THERE ANYTHING ELSE YOU WANT TO SHARE, FOREMAN? DID THE JEDI SABOTAGE ANY OF OUR SHIPS?
NO, BUT THEY DO HAVE REINFORCEMENTS ON THE PLATEAU IN HIDING. OVERSEER...THE JEDI MERELY WANTED TO LEAD US IN ESCAPE.

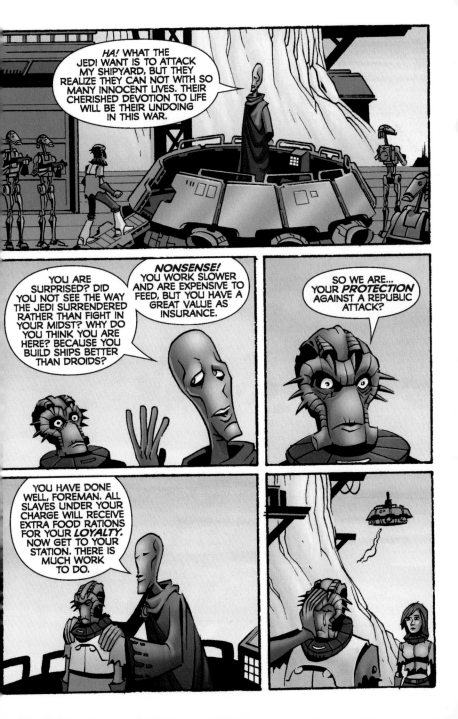

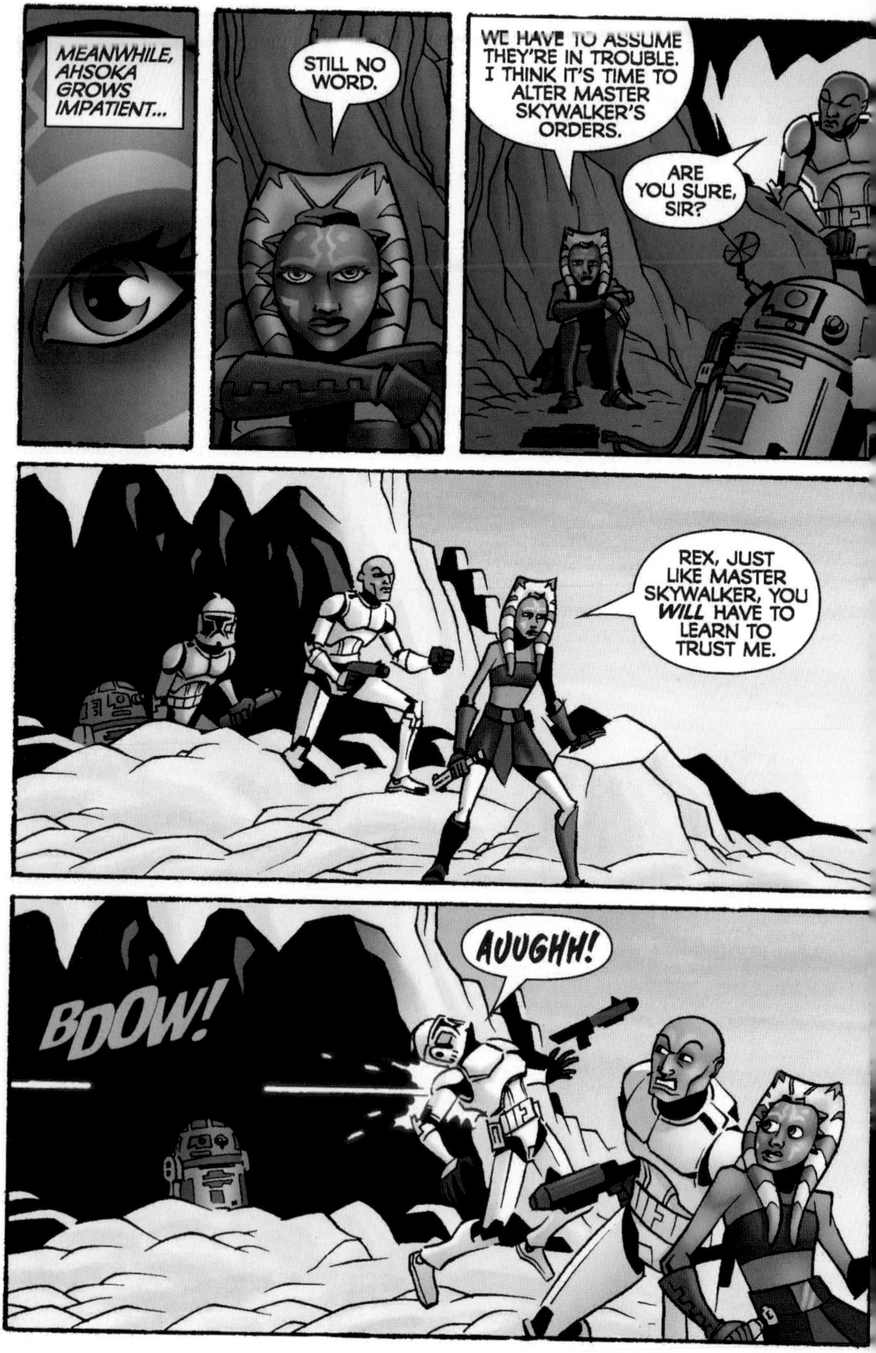

MEANWHILE, AHSOKA GROWS IMPATIENT...
STILL NO WORD.
WE HAVE TO ASSUME THEY'RE IN TROUBLE. I THINK IT'S TIME TO ALTER MASTER SKYWALKER'S ORDERS.
ARE YOU SURE, SIR?
REX, JUST LIKE MASTER SKYWALKER, YOU WILL HAVE TO LEARN TO TRUST ME.
BDOW!
AUUGHH!

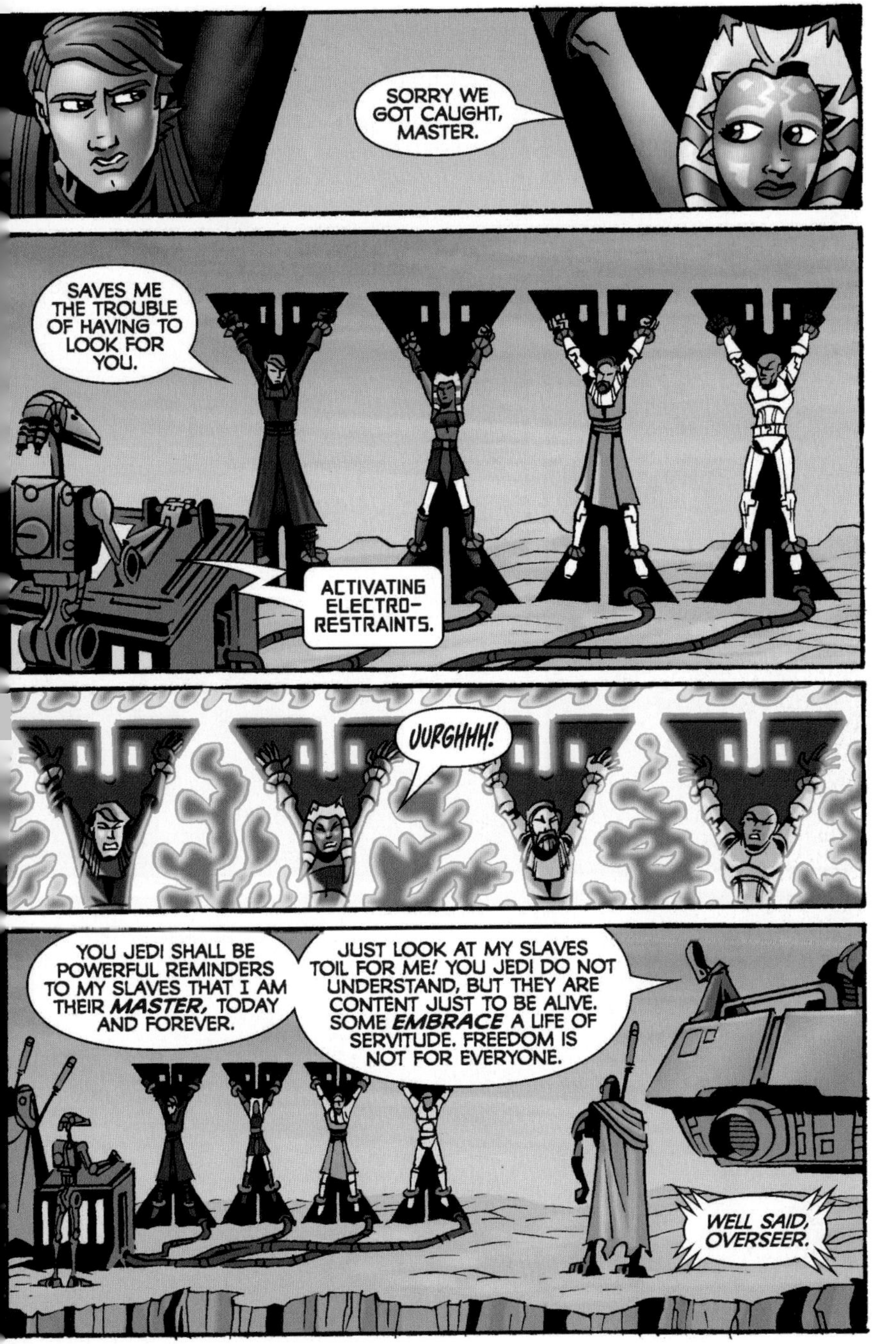
SORRY WE GOT CAUGHT, MASTER.
SAVES ME THE TROUBLE OF HAVING TO LOOK FOR YOU.
ACTIVATING ELECTRO-RESTRAINTS.
UURGHHH!
YOU JEDI SHALL BE POWERFUL REMINDERS TO MY SLAVES THAT I AM THEIR MASTER, TODAY AND FOREVER.
JUST LOOK AT MY SLAVES TOIL FOR ME! YOU JEDI DO NOT UNDERSTAND, BUT THEY ARE CONTENT JUST TO BE ALIVE. SOME EMBRACE A LIFE OF SERVITUDE. FREEDOM IS NOT FOR EVERYONE.
WELL SAID, OVERSEER.

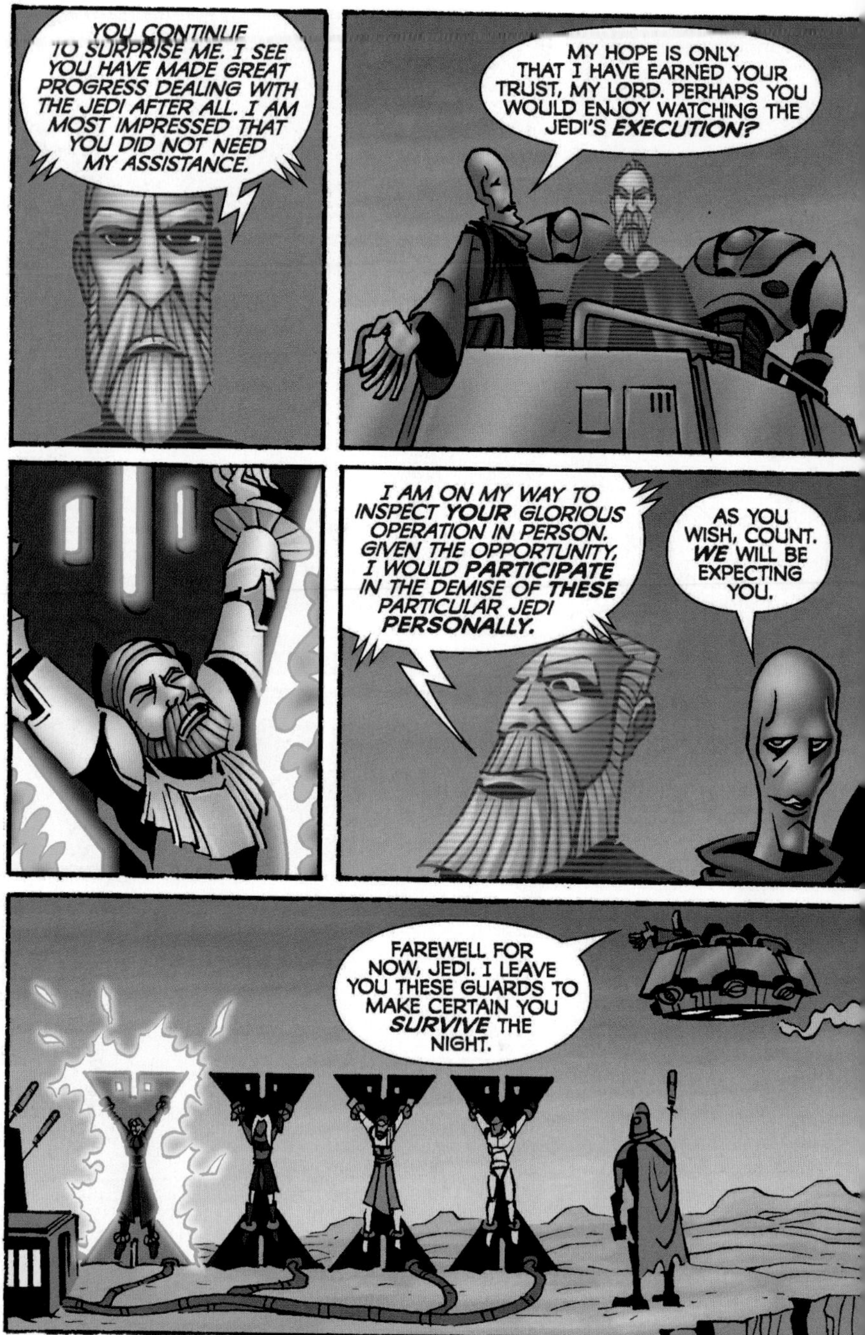
YOU CONTINUE TO SURPRISE ME. I SEE YOU HAVE MADE GREAT PROGRESS DEALING WITH THE JEDI AFTER ALL. I AM MOST IMPRESSED THAT YOU DID NOT NEED MY ASSISTANCE.
MY HOPE IS ONLY THAT I HAVE EARNED YOUR TRUST, MY LORD. PERHAPS YOU WOULD ENJOY WATCHING THE JEDI'S EXECUTION?
I AM ON MY WAY TO INSPECT YOUR GLORIOUS OPERATION IN PERSON. GIVEN THE OPPORTUNITY, I WOULD PARTICIPATE IN THE DEMISE OF THESE PARTICULAR JEDI PERSONALLY.
AS YOU WISH, COUNT. WE WILL BE EXPECTING YOU.
FAREWELL FOR NOW, JEDI. I LEAVE YOU THESE GUARDS TO MAKE CERTAIN YOU SURVIVE THE NIGHT.

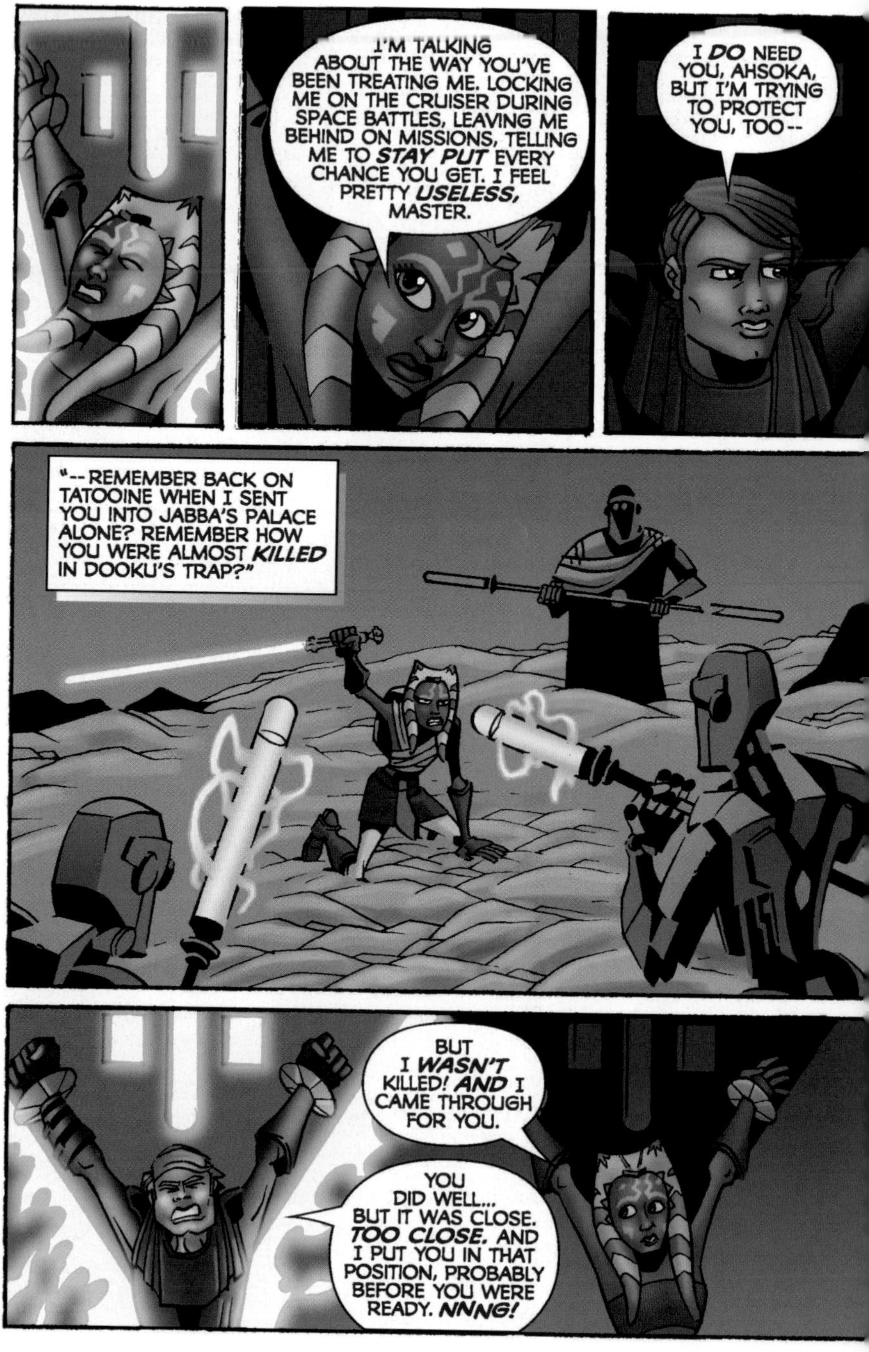
I'M TALKING ABOUT THE WAY YOU'VE BEEN TREATING ME. LOCKING ME ON THE CRUISER DURING SPACE BATTLES, LEAVING ME BEHIND ON MISSIONS, TELLING ME TO STAY PUT EVERY CHANCE YOU GET. I FEEL PRETTY USELESS, MASTER.
I DO NEED YOU, AHSOKA, BUT I'M TRYING TO PROTECT YOU, TOO--
"--REMEMBER BACK ON TATOOINE WHEN I SENT YOU INTO JABBA'S PALACE ALONE? REMEMBER HOW YOU WERE ALMOST KILLED IN DOOKU'S TRAP?"
BUT I WASN'T KILLED! AND I CAME THROUGH FOR YOU.
YOU DID WELL... BUT IT WAS CLOSE. TOO CLOSE. AND I PUT YOU IN THAT POSITION, PROBABLY BEFORE YOU WERE READY. NNNG!

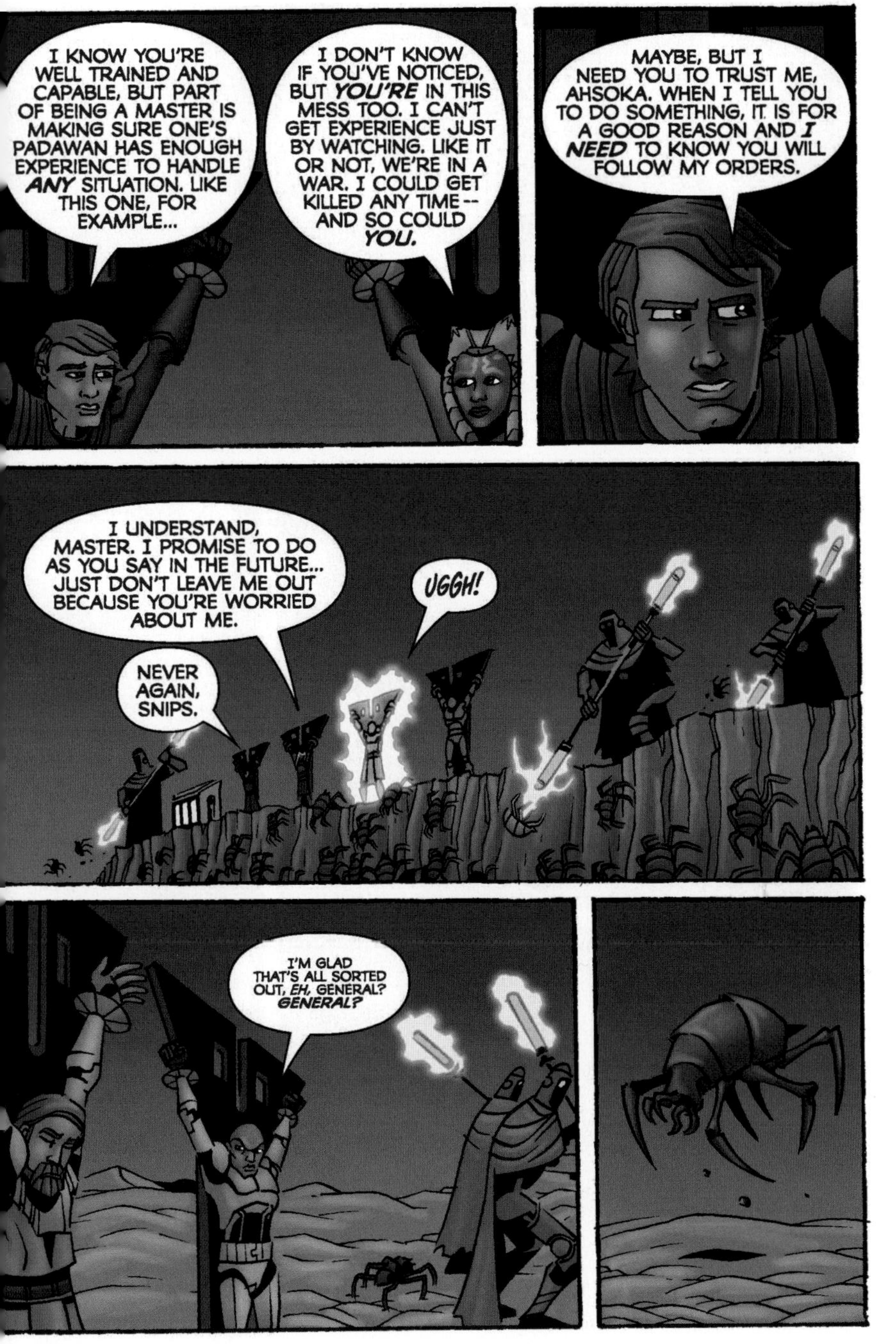

I KNOW YOU'RE WELL TRAINED AND CAPABLE, BUT PART OF BEING A MASTER IS MAKING SURE ONE'S PADAWAN HAS ENOUGH EXPERIENCE TO HANDLE *ANY* SITUATION. LIKE THIS ONE, FOR EXAMPLE...
I DON'T KNOW IF YOU'VE NOTICED, BUT *YOU'RE* IN THIS MESS TOO. I CAN'T GET EXPERIENCE JUST BY WATCHING. LIKE IT OR NOT, WE'RE IN A WAR. I COULD GET KILLED ANY TIME -- AND SO COULD *YOU.*
MAYBE, BUT I NEED YOU TO TRUST ME, AHSOKA. WHEN I TELL YOU TO DO SOMETHING, IT IS FOR A GOOD REASON AND *I NEED* TO KNOW YOU WILL FOLLOW MY ORDERS.
I UNDERSTAND, MASTER. I PROMISE TO DO AS YOU SAY IN THE FUTURE... JUST DON'T LEAVE ME OUT BECAUSE YOU'RE WORRIED ABOUT ME.
UGGH!
NEVER AGAIN, SNIPS.
I'M GLAD THAT'S ALL SORTED OUT, *EH,* GENERAL? *GENERAL?*

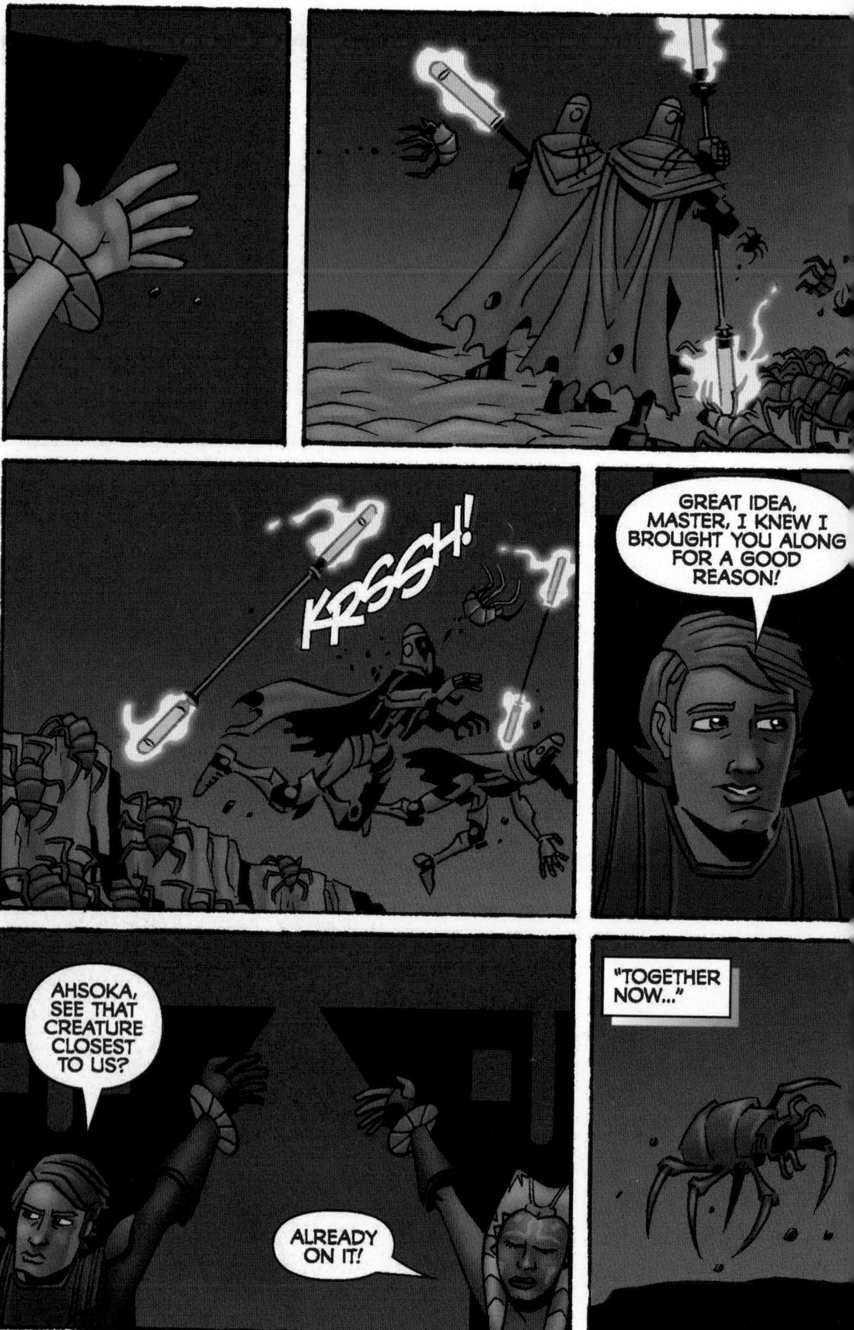
KRSSH!
GREAT IDEA, MASTER, I KNEW I BROUGHT YOU ALONG FOR A GOOD REASON!
AHSOKA, SEE THAT CREATURE CLOSEST TO US?
ALREADY ON IT!
"TOGETHER NOW..."

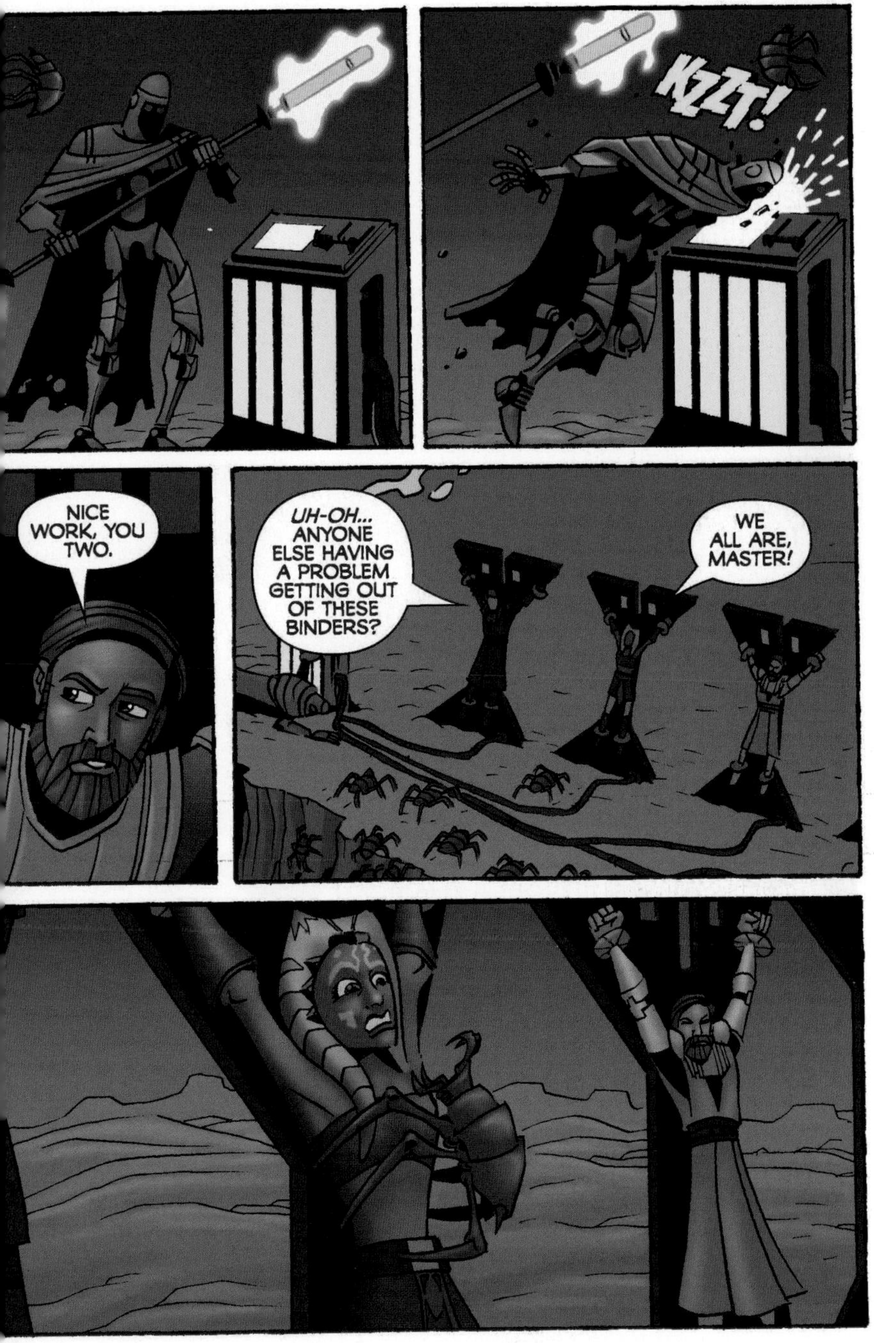
KZZT!
NICE WORK, YOU TWO.
UH-OH... ANYONE ELSE HAVING A PROBLEM GETTING OUT OF THESE BINDERS?
WE ALL ARE, MASTER!

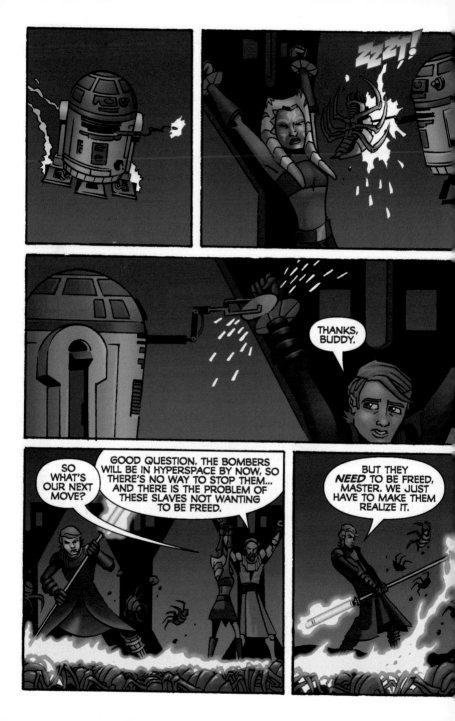

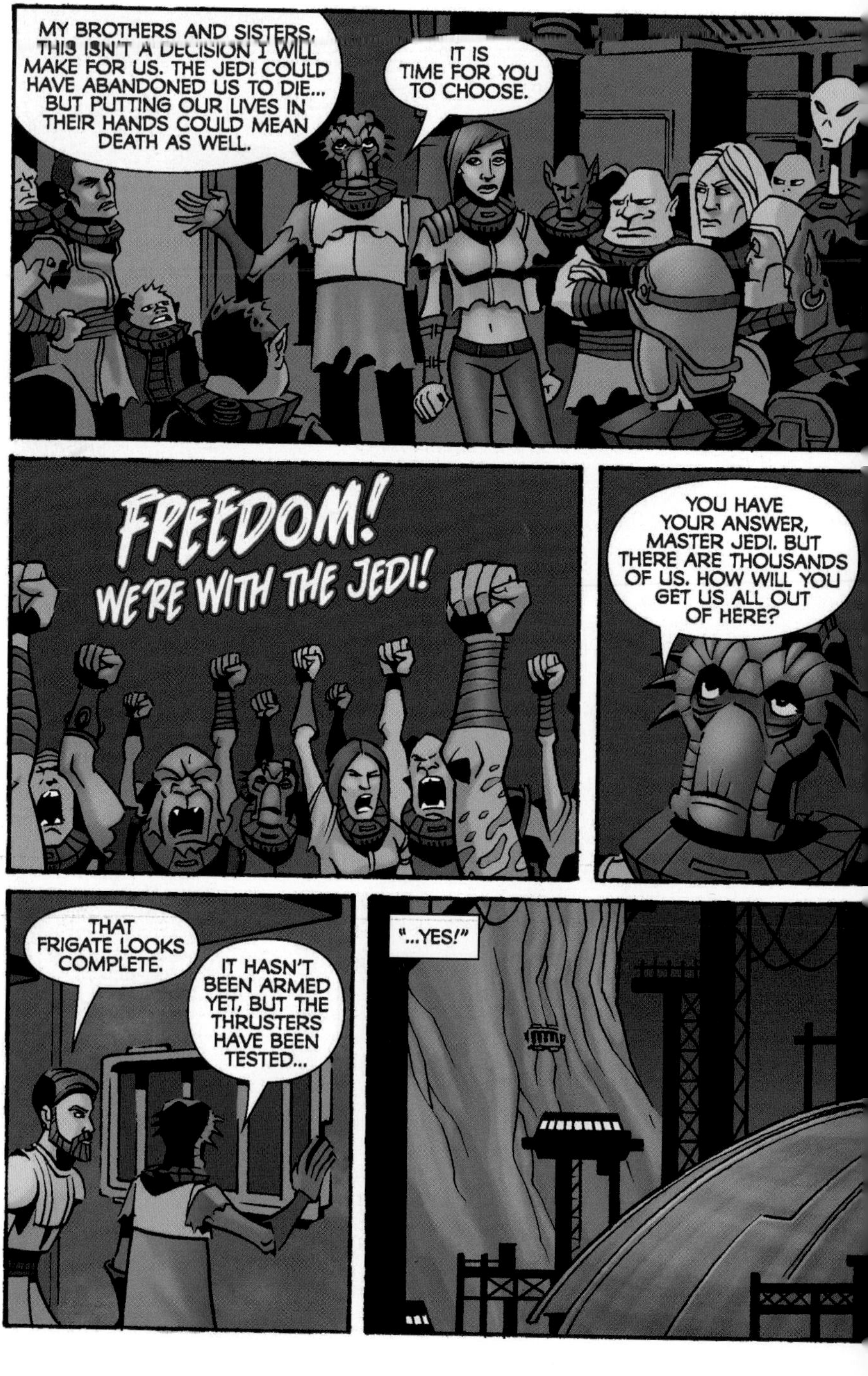
MY BROTHERS AND SISTERS, THIS ISN'T A DECISION I WILL MAKE FOR US. THE JEDI COULD HAVE ABANDONED US TO DIE... BUT PUTTING OUR LIVES IN THEIR HANDS COULD MEAN DEATH AS WELL.
IT IS TIME FOR YOU TO CHOOSE.
FREEDOM!
WE'RE WITH THE JEDI!
YOU HAVE YOUR ANSWER, MASTER JEDI. BUT THERE ARE THOUSANDS OF US. HOW WILL YOU GET US ALL OUT OF HERE?
THAT FRIGATE LOOKS COMPLETE.
IT HASN'T BEEN ARMED YET, BUT THE THRUSTERS HAVE BEEN TESTED...
"...YES!"

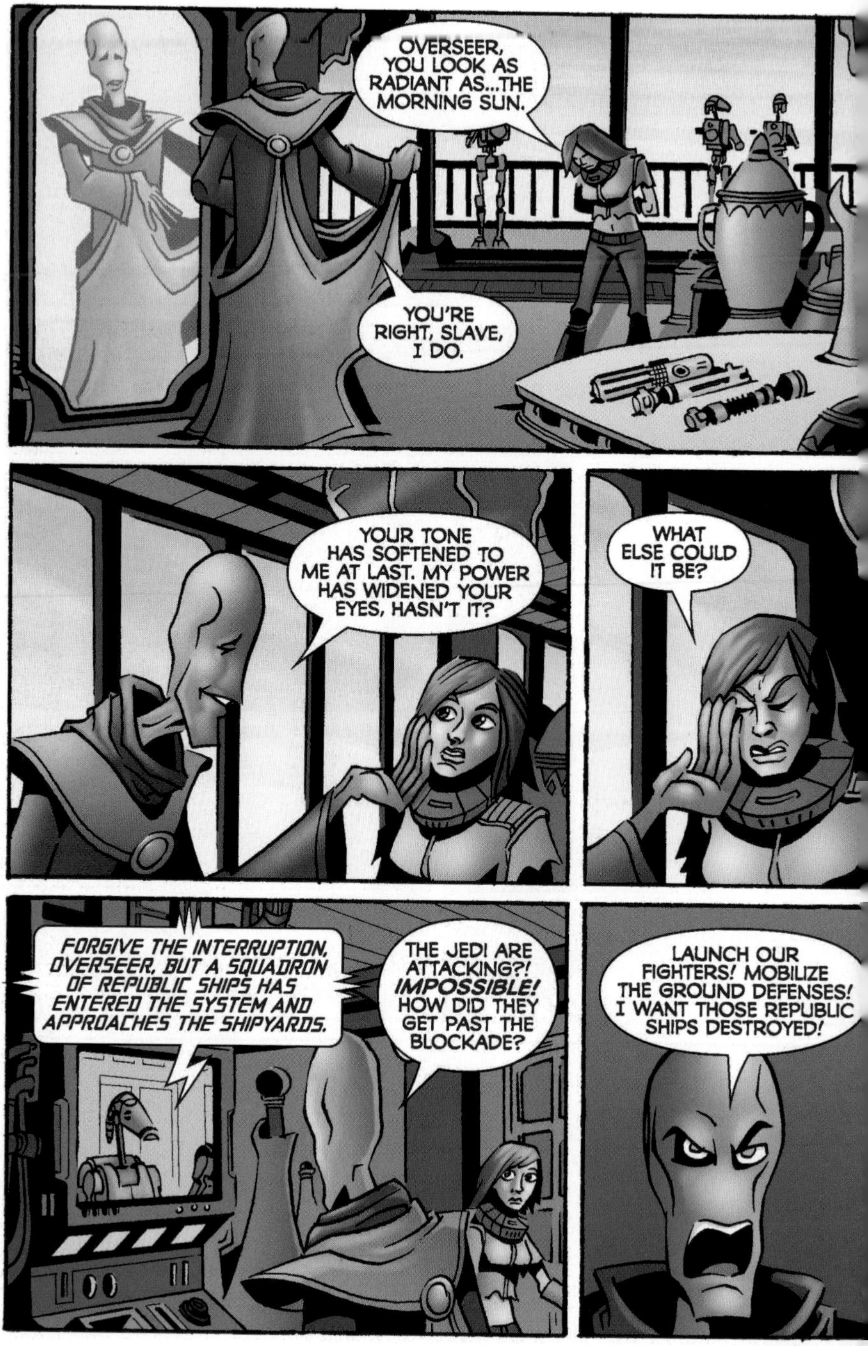
OVERSEER, YOU LOOK AS RADIANT AS...THE MORNING SUN.
YOU'RE RIGHT, SLAVE, I DO.
YOUR TONE HAS SOFTENED TO ME AT LAST. MY POWER HAS WIDENED YOUR EYES, HASN'T IT?
WHAT ELSE COULD IT BE?
FORGIVE THE INTERRUPTION, OVERSEER, BUT A SQUADRON OF REPUBLIC SHIPS HAS ENTERED THE SYSTEM AND APPROACHES THE SHIPYARDS.
THE JEDI ARE ATTACKING?! *IMPOSSIBLE!* HOW DID THEY GET PAST THE BLOCKADE?
LAUNCH OUR FIGHTERS! MOBILIZE THE GROUND DEFENSES! I WANT THOSE REPUBLIC SHIPS DESTROYED!

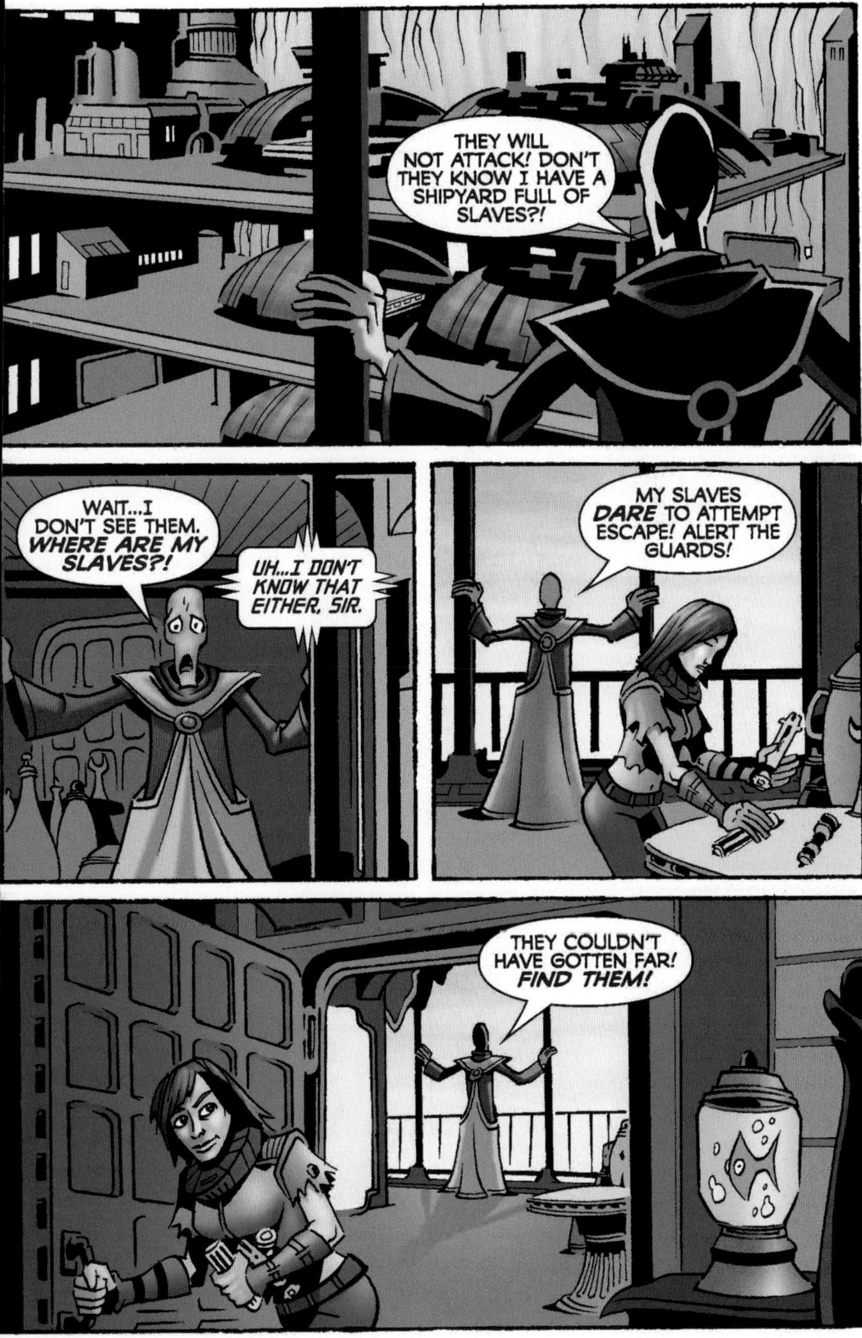
THEY WILL NOT ATTACK! DON'T THEY KNOW I HAVE A SHIPYARD FULL OF SLAVES?!
WAIT...I DON'T SEE THEM. *WHERE ARE MY SLAVES?!*
UH...I DON'T KNOW THAT EITHER, SIR.
MY SLAVES *DARE* TO ATTEMPT ESCAPE! ALERT THE GUARDS!
THEY COULDN'T HAVE GOTTEN FAR! *FIND THEM!*

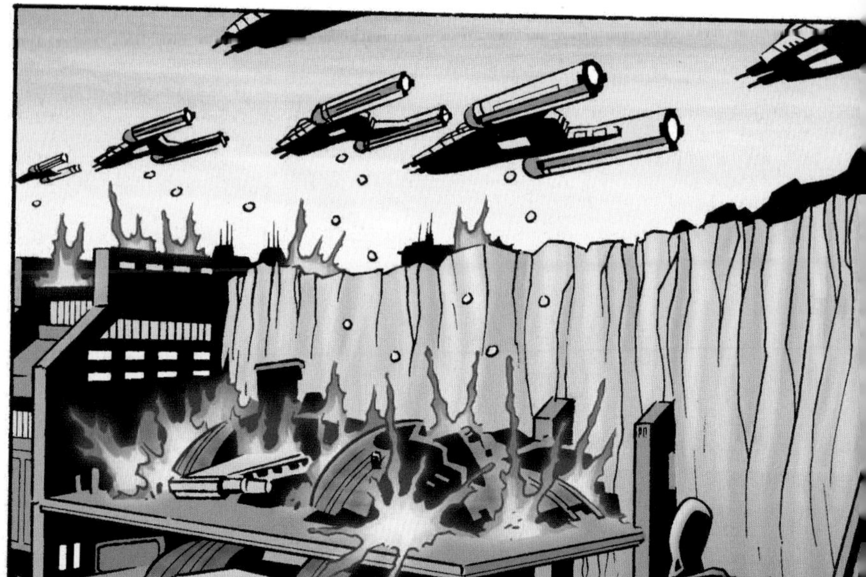
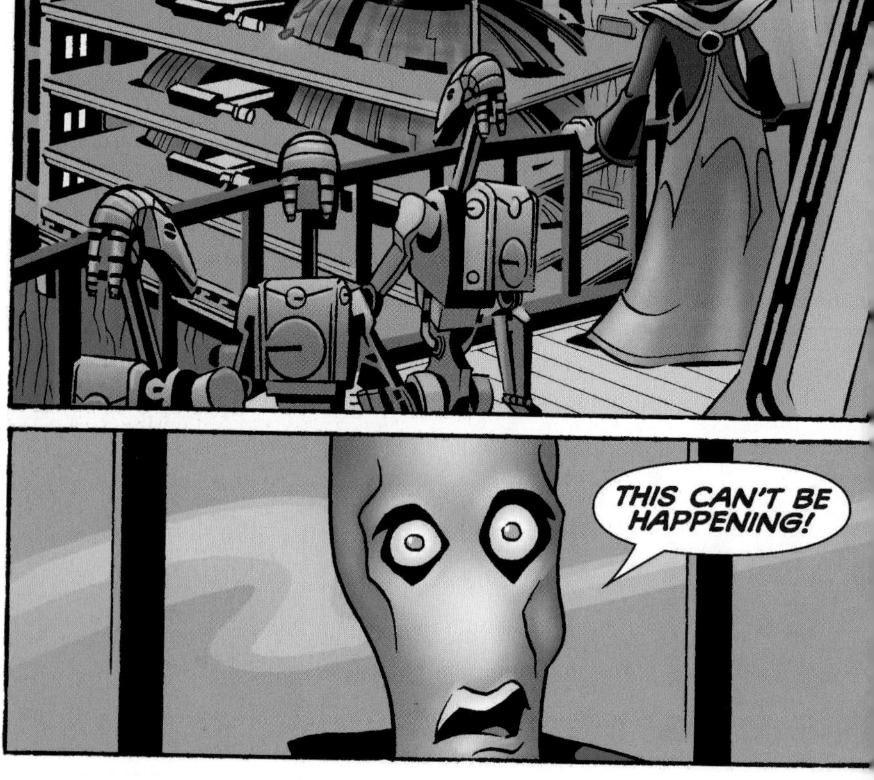
THIS CAN'T BE HAPPENING!

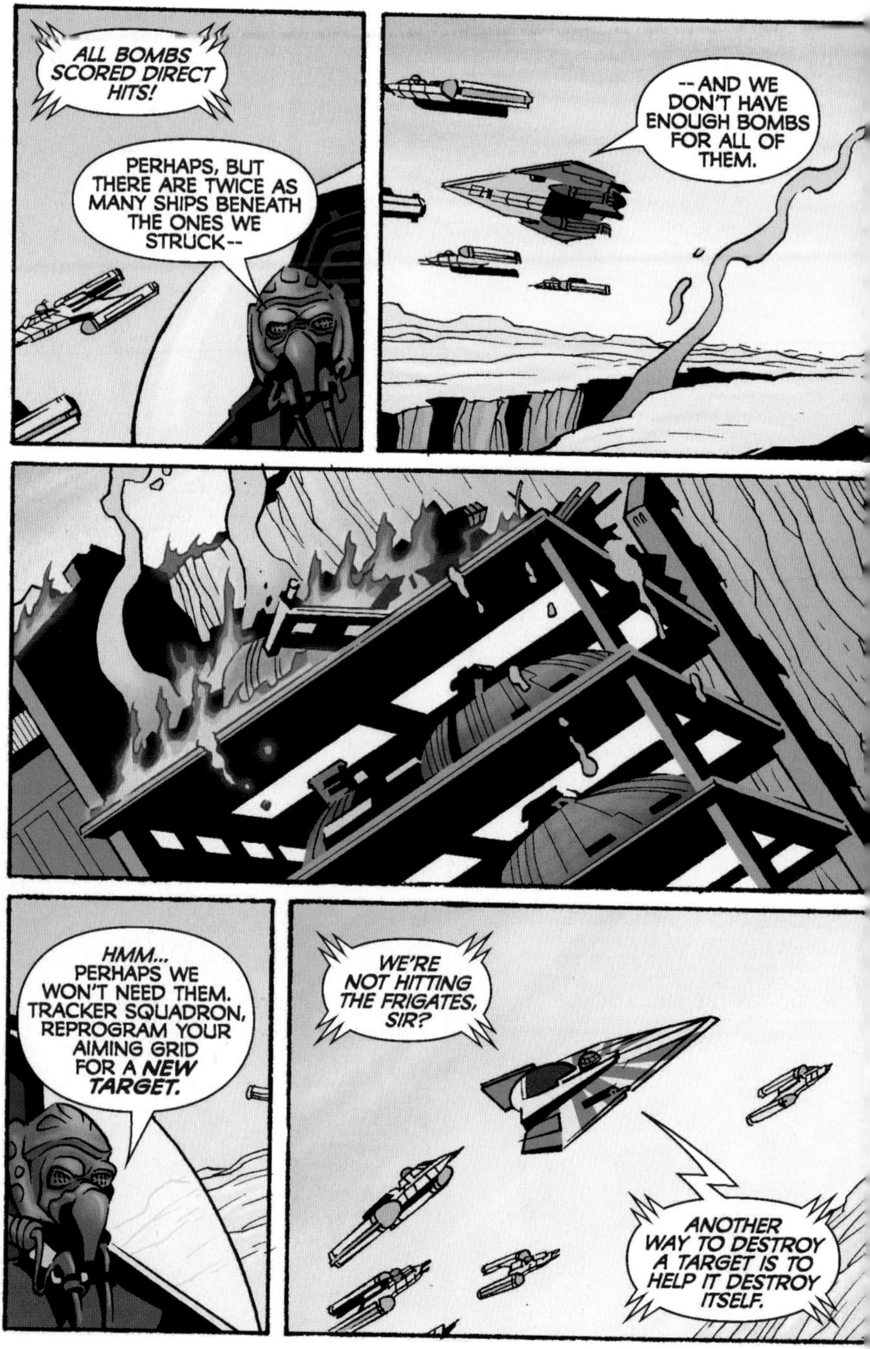
ALL BOMBS SCORED DIRECT HITS!
PERHAPS, BUT THERE ARE TWICE AS MANY SHIPS BENEATH THE ONES WE STRUCK--
--AND WE DON'T HAVE ENOUGH BOMBS FOR ALL OF THEM.
HMM... PERHAPS WE WON'T NEED THEM. TRACKER SQUADRON, REPROGRAM YOUR AIMING GRID FOR A NEW TARGET.
WE'RE NOT HITTING THE FRIGATES, SIR?
ANOTHER WAY TO DESTROY A TARGET IS TO HELP IT DESTROY ITSELF.

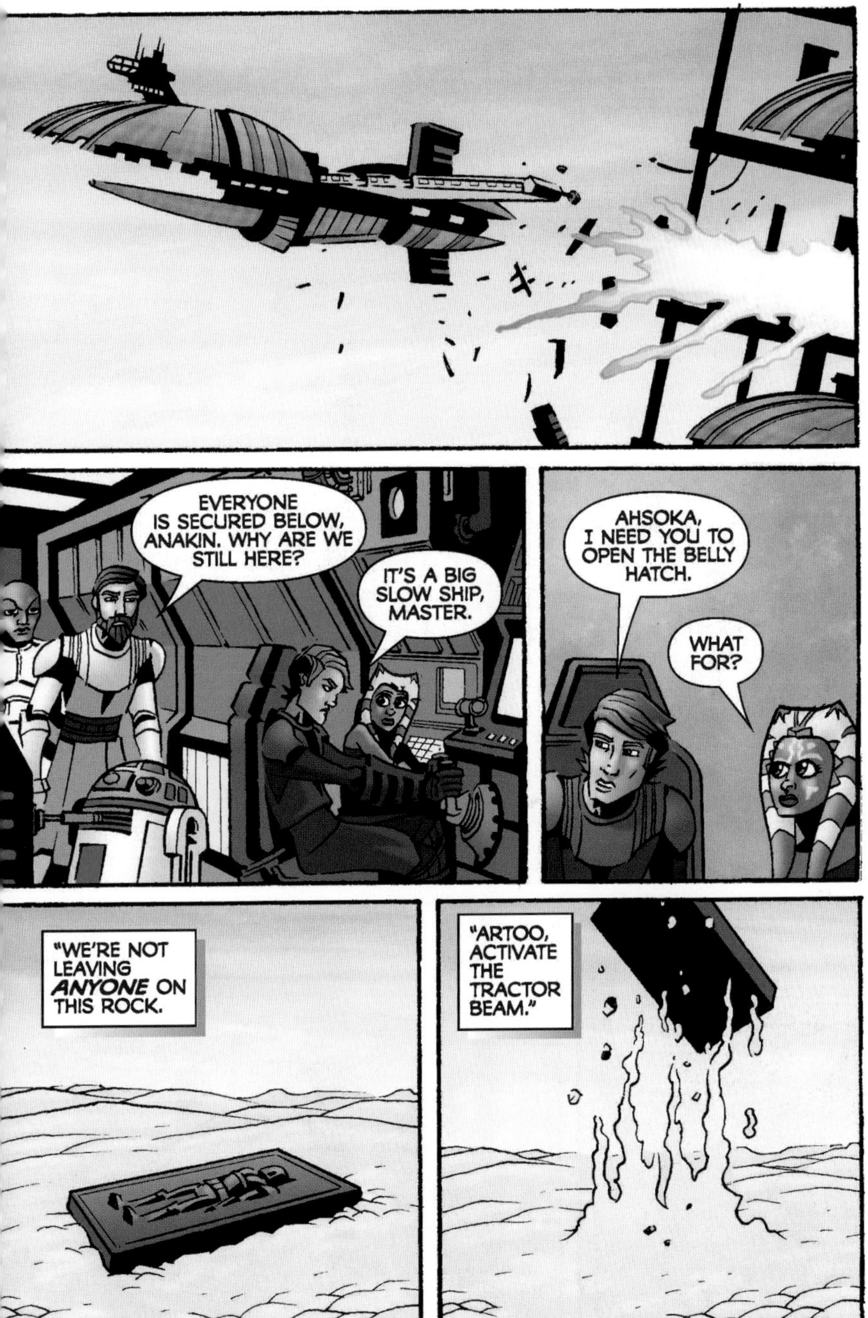
EVERYONE IS SECURED BELOW, ANAKIN. WHY ARE WE STILL HERE?
IT'S A BIG SLOW SHIP, MASTER.
AHSOKA, I NEED YOU TO OPEN THE BELLY HATCH.
WHAT FOR?
"WE'RE NOT LEAVING *ANYONE* ON THIS ROCK.
"ARTOO, ACTIVATE THE TRACTOR BEAM."

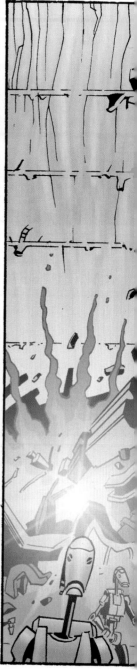

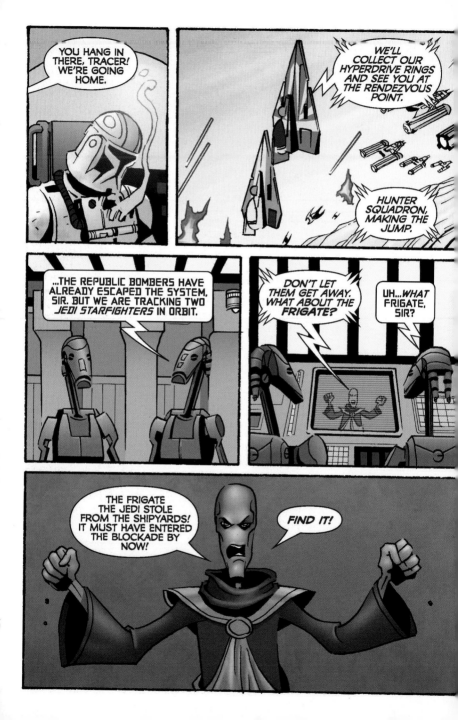

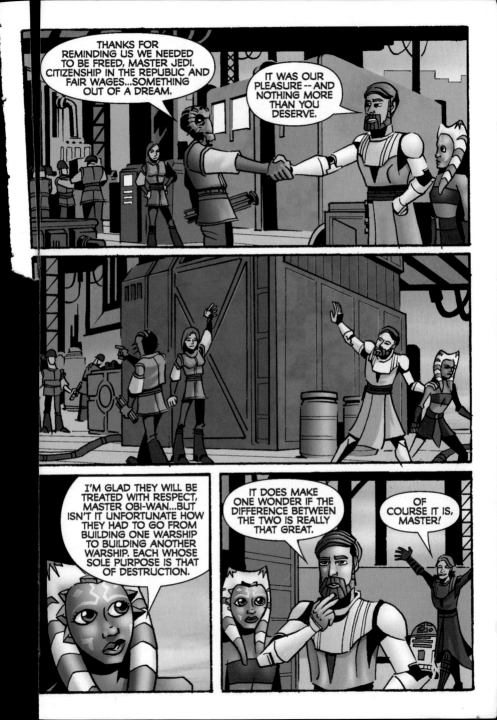

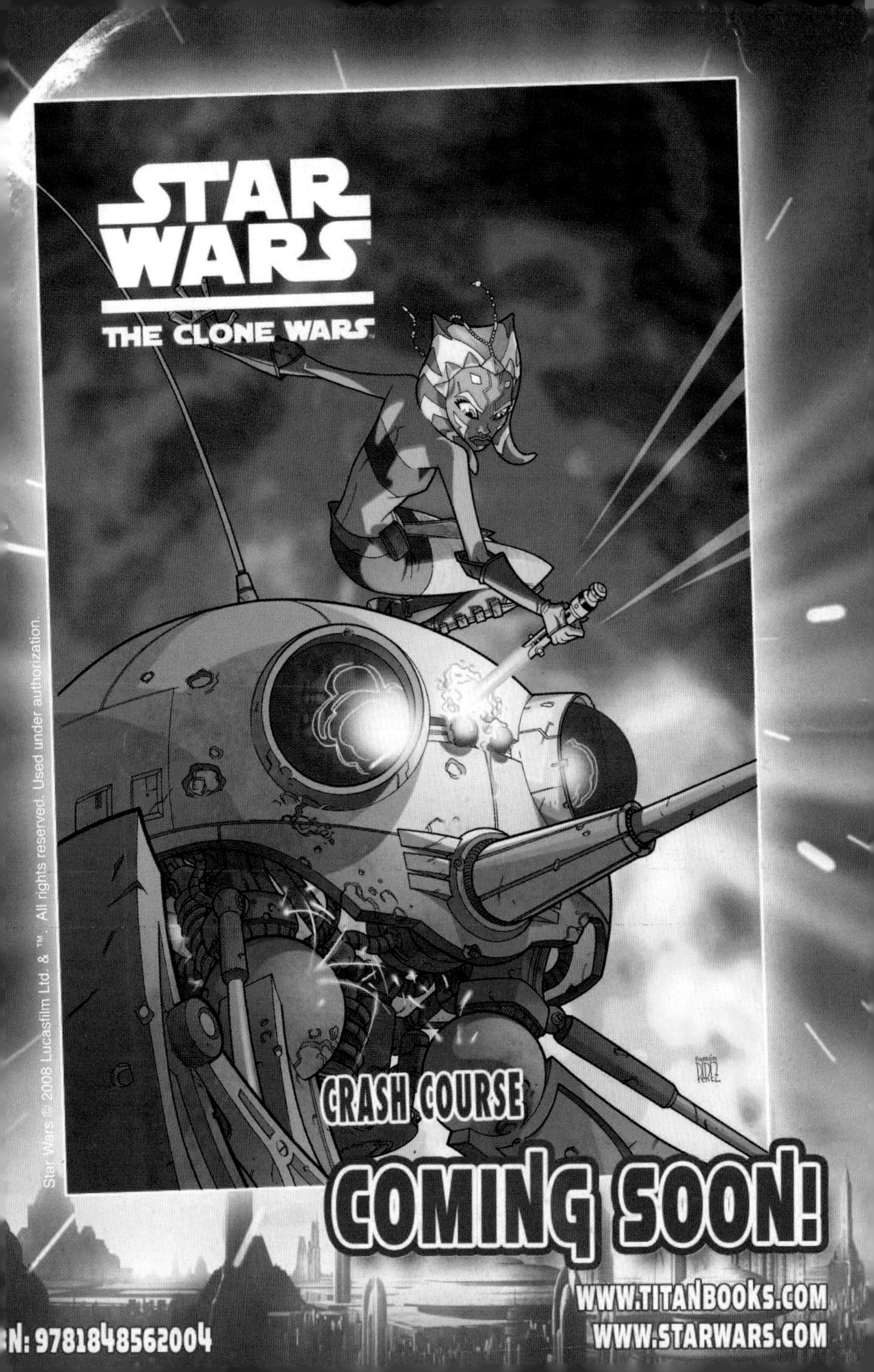
STAR WARS
THE CLONE WARS
CRASH COURSE
COMING SOON!
N: 9781848562004
WWW.TITANBOOKS.COM
WWW.STARWARS.COM

THE FORCE I9

DON'T MISS THE CONTINUING BATTLE AGAIN

CLONE WARS

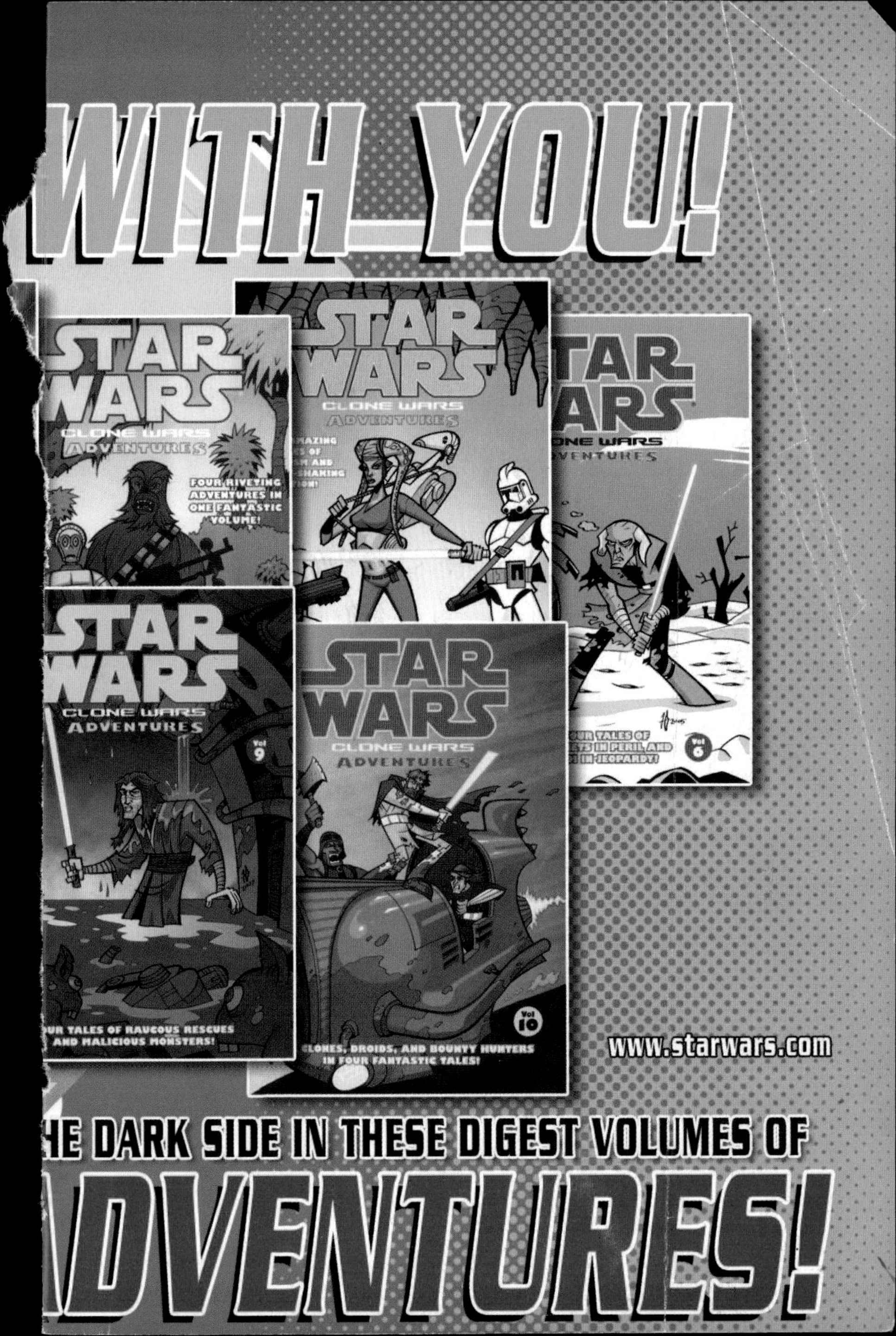
WITH YOU!
STAR WARS
CLONE WARS
ADVENTURES
FOUR RIVETING ADVENTURES IN ONE FANTASTIC VOLUME!
STAR WARS
CLONE WARS
ADVENTURES
STAR WARS
CLONE WARS
ADVENTURES
STAR WARS
CLONE WARS
ADVENTURES
Vol 9
OUR TALES OF RAUCOUS RESCUES AND MALICIOUS MONSTERS!
STAR WARS
CLONE WARS
ADVENTURES
Vol 10
CLONES, DROIDS, AND BOUNTY HUNTERS IN FOUR FANTASTIC TALES!
Vol 6
www.starwars.com
HE DARK SIDE IN THESE DIGEST VOLUMES OF
DVENTURES!

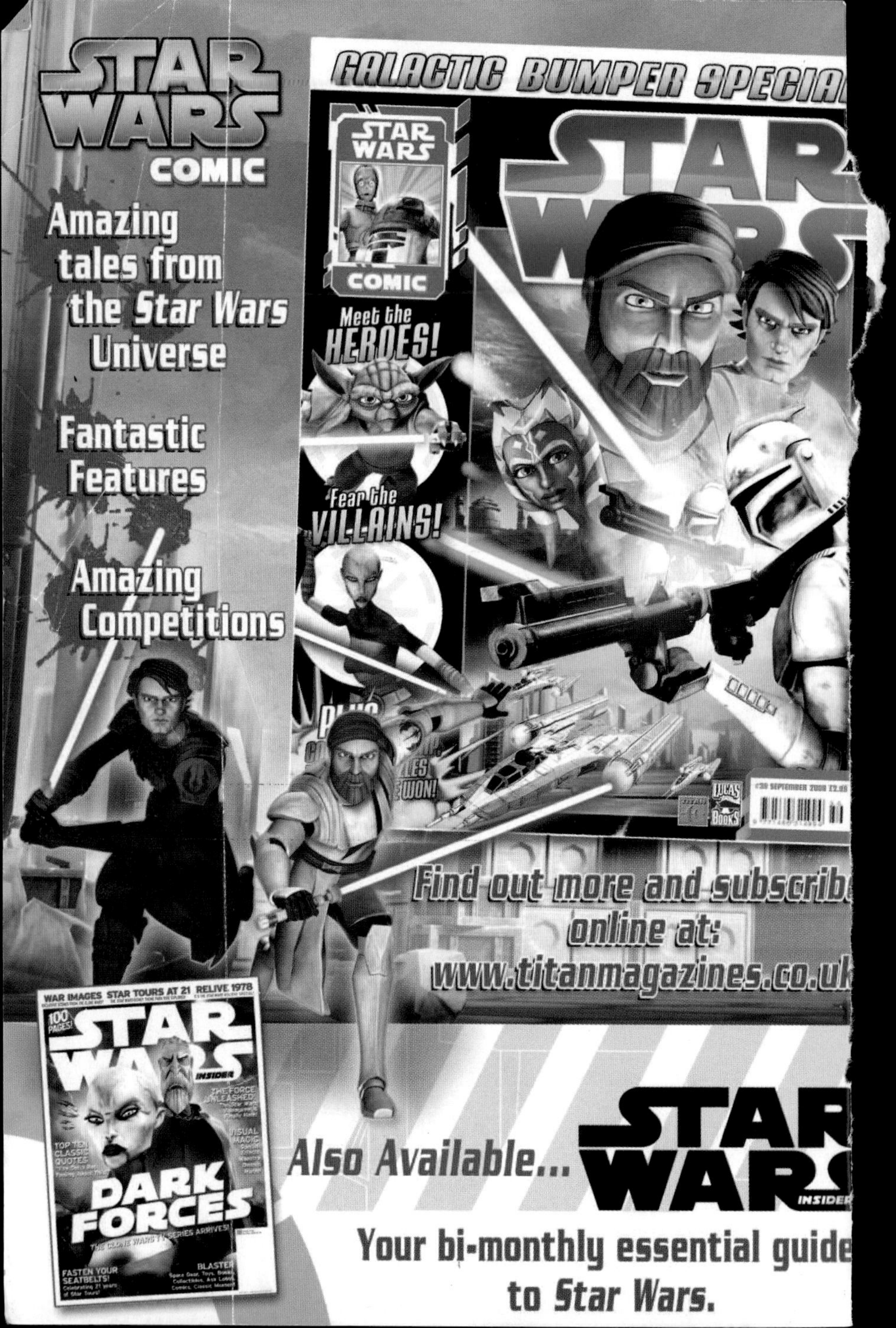

STAR WARS COMIC
Amazing tales from the Star Wars Universe
Fantastic Features
Amazing Competitions
GALACTIC BUMPER SPECIA
STAR WARS COMIC
Meet the HEROES!
Fear the VILLAINS!
Find out more and subscrib
online at:
www.titanmagazines.co.uk
WAR IMAGES STAR TOURS AT 21 RELIVE 1978
100 PAGES!
STAR WARS INSIDER
THE FORCE UNLEASHED
TOP TEN CLASSIC QUOTES
VISUAL MAGIC
DARK FORCES
THE CLONE WARS TV SERIES ARRIVES!
FASTEN YOUR SEATBELTS!
BLASTER
Also Available...
STAR WARS INSIDER
Your bi-monthly essential guide
to Star Wars.